MW00973547

History And Profiles By Eugene N. Zeigler

Produced in cooperation with the
Greater Florence Chamber of Commerce
610 West Palmetto Street
P.O. Box 948
Florence, South Carolina 29503
(803) 665-0515

Foreword

On behalf of the Board of Directors of the Greater Florence Chamber of Commerce, I am pleased to present to you *Florence: A Renaissance Spirit.* This work drew upon the skills of many dedicated people within the community and within Community Communications. Special thanks go to author Nick Zeigler and to Dr. G. Wayne King for sharing photographs from his collection. Wayne Terry, (Cherry, Bekeart & Holland) treasurer of the Chamber, and Susan Farver, vice president of the Chamber, have overseen this project from the beginning. Many businesses and individuals have made major contributions; some are recognized within the book, others have done so without recognition.

Florence County developed as the result of many men and women whose families settled throughout this region when it was the frontier of an English colony. These people led a strenuous life to cultivate this frontier land and establish a place for themselves and their families. Farming and timber were their first enterprises. Today, businesses like farming and timber, banks, retail stores, and services have been in families for generations.

Many of the settlements became towns. Today there are nine incorporated municipalities in Florence County: Coward, Florence, Johnsonville, Lake City, Olanta, Pamplico, Quinby, Scranton, and Timmonsville. Each of these towns has its own splendid and colorful history, a history as vibrant as its citizens. Unfortunately, space does not allow the telling of each story in detail. Perhaps their histories will be the making of another book. The current towns in order of their creation are as follows:

Lake City–Settled about 1732 by Scotch-Irish, to whom land was granted to develop the back country of Charlestown and Beaufort, the first name given was The Crossroads. The town later became known as McCrea's Crossroads, Graham's Crossroads, Lynch's Lake, and finally Lake City. The name Lake City was derived from two popular fishing and swimming lakes located just north of town. After the Civil War, settling refugees made the area grow rapidly and become the hub of the agricultural economy of the region.

Coward–In the 1790s the area was settled by William McGee, who cleared land for his log cabin. Originally, the settlement was called Lynch. The name was later changed to Coward in honor of Asbury Coward, a native son, who became commander of the Citadel Military College in Charleston, South Carolina.

Olanta–Known as Beulah Crossroads for many years, the area was settled in the early 1800s. Olanta was officially chartered in 1908. From the 1930s to the

1950s the area thrived as a cotton buying market. With five churches and a city population of less than 700 persons, Olanta has one of the highest church-per-person populations anywhere.

Timmonsville–In 1831 the governor of South Carolina granted Rev. James Morgan Timmons 1,384 acres of land for less than two dollars per acre. He built a steam-operated saw and grist mill, a turpentine still, a store, a three-story dwelling, and the first railroad depot. Timmons became prosperous, purchased additional land, and helped the area grow.

Johnsonville–Originally this town was a small community on the bluff of Lynches River, where Witherspoon's Ferry (later known as Johnson's Ferry) had been established. Although the post office was established in 1843, which was named Johnsonville, it was not until 1912, immediately after the railroad came through, that an actual town developed.

Scranton–The first store and house was built in 1852 in the town of Scranton (then called Myersville). The town name was later changed to Leesville, then finally to Scranton. The name Scranton originated with two lumbermen who came to the town from Scranton, Pennsylvania, to set up a lumber mill.

Florence–Established as a railroad depot in 1853 and named for the daughter of the first president of the railroad, this sometimes raucous town has grown to become the hub of the region.

Pamplico–Although settled in the 1800s, Pamplico was not incorporated until 1916.

Quinby–The newest city in Florence County, Quinby was chartered in 1967 and incorporated in 1976. Quinby was formed when the residential subdivisions of Quinby Estates and Quinby Forest merged. The first mayor was Ashby Gregg Sr. His son, Ashby Gregg Jr., is mayor today.

The same enterprising spirit which helped to settle and develop the Florence County region is thriving today. We are proud to be a part of it. We dedicate this book to those individuals who have worked to provide our community with its vibrancy and high quality of life.

J. David Wansley
President
Greater Florence Chamber of Commerce
June 18, 1996

This Centennial Celebration announcement features the fleur-de-lis, part of the county's official seal.

Preface

The Industrial Revolution brought Florence into being. In 1857 the junction of three railroads in a pine forest located in the approximate center of the Pee Dee region of South Carolina created a village. Within 15 years, years that saw the South transformed by the Civil War, that village became a town and, within 20 years, a county seat. In 1890 Florence was incorporated as a city, and in the ensuing years has grown to become the industrial, commercial, and cultural center of the Pee Dee region.

The Pee Dee region of South Carolina comprises about one fifth of the area of the state's northeastern corner. It is generally defined as being composed of the nine counties bordering the Great Pee Dee River: Chesterfield, Marlboro, Dillon, Darlington, Florence, Marion, Williamsburg, Horry, and Georgetown. Only Dillon County, created in 1910, is younger than Florence. Unlike Dillon, however, Florence County's formation was powered by forces new to the South in the decades after the Civil War. These forces transformed Florence, a town and city in the heart of the Old South, into something that was a phenomenon of the New. As a result, Florence has, throughout its history, stood in marked contrast with the social and economic realities of the antebellum South, and in the last century and a quarter its progress has been an index of the fortunes of a South that has once again come to national prominence.

The story of the evolution of Florence is thus quite different from that of its neighboring cities. Florence, at the end of the last century, was more like a western than a southern town. It was a place of economic opportunity and social mobility in the midst of a society torn apart by war. References to it as the "Gate City" and the "Magic City" may have been appropriate at the time they were made; however, Florence's development as a metropolitan center is more a story of rebirth and regeneration. Seen now in the perspective of more than a hundred years, Florence is, as its name unintentionally implies, a "Renaissance City." It has succeeded in combining, and it continues to combine, the best of the Old South and the New–heritage, hope, and renewal in a world of constant change.

Eugene N. Zeigler

Community Communications, Inc.
Publishers: Ronald P. Beers and James E. Turner

Staff for *Florence: A Renaissance Spirit*
Publisher's Sales Associate: Marie Perdue
Executive Editor: James E. Turner
Managing Editor: Linda Moeller Pegram
Design Director: Camille Leonard
Designer: Scott Phillips
Photo Editors: Linda M. Pegram and Scott Phillips
Production Manager: Corinne Cau
Editorial Assistant: Katrina Williams
Sales Assistant: Annette R. Lozier
Proofreader: Wynona B. Hall
Accounting Services: Sara Ann Turner
Printing Production: Frank Rosenberg/GSAmerica

Community Communications, Inc.
Montgomery, Alabama

James E. Turner, Chairman of the Board
Ronald P. Beers, President
Daniel S. Chambliss, Vice President

Published 1996
Printed in the United States of America
First Edition
Library of Congress Catalog Number: 96-42246
ISBN: 1-885352-48-4

Table of Contents

Chapter One

The Colonial and Antebellum Background

(1734-1846)

Colonel Francis Marion crossing the Pee Dee River, circa 1790. This painting was done in 1850 by William Ranney. A copy done in 1857 is owned by the Florence Museum.

Saint David's Church in Cheraw, South Carolina. Built in 1772, it is the oldest existing building in the Pee Dee region built with public funds.

When the Europeans settled what is now South Carolina, the inhabitants of the Pee Dee region were members of the Siouxan nation, represented by the Waccamaws in the coastal area and the Pedee and Cheraw tribes in the interior. The name of the river and of the tribe is thought to come from the word *piri* in the Siouxan language, which means "something good." Generally, "Pee Dee" was written as one word in colonial records but was given several different spellings. In the 1940s, it was, by common consent, spelled as two words, "Pee Dee."

It is estimated that there were 600 members of the "Pedee" tribe in 1600; however, after contact with Europeans, their numbers had dwindled as a result of disease, alcoholism, and the encroachment of white settlers. By the time of the Revolutionary War, the surviving remnants were absorbed into the population or had become part of the Catawba Nation, another Siouxan tribe in what is now York County, South Carolina, where their descendants still live.

In 1670 the English settlement at Charles Town (later Charleston) established the center of all activity until the 1770s. Following the trauma of the Yemasee Indian War (1715), and the transfer of the government from the Lords Proprietors to the English crown (1719), the first royal governor initiated what was known as the township program in which "poor Protestants" were invited to settle in the back country and encouraged to do so by offering them grants of land.

The early settlers of the Pee Dee came as a part of this township program and comprised three separate groups. First, in 1732, Williamsburg Township brought Scotch-Irish Presbyterian settlers and began the spread of the Presbyterian Church. Second, came the English, who were generally members of the Anglican Church. Theirs was the Parish of Prince Frederick on Black River, extended in 1734 by the creation of Prince George Parish in Georgetown, which was becoming a prosperous port near the mouth of the Pee Dee River at Winyah Bay. Third, in 1736, Welsh Baptists in Pennsylvania petitioned to buy all vacant land along the upper Pee Dee. They settled in the area of Society Hill in Darlington County, and from this settlement originated most of the Baptist churches in the Pee Dee.

During this time the Pee Dee River and its tributaries were the main routes for transportation into the region. There were few serviceable roads. The "River Road," on the western side of the Pee Dee River, followed an Indian trading path from Georgetown to Cheraw. After the rivers, it was the most important means of communication with the back country, and like roads to the west of the Pee Dee, it was accessible only by ferry.

The "Indian Trade" was one of the means to making a fortune in the early days of the colony. The principal "paths" from Charles Town to the Indian country led south and west in the direction of the Creek nation in what is now Georgia, and northwest to the Cherokee nation in upper South Carolina, North Carolina, and Tennessee. Thus, the Pee Dee region was something of a commercial backwater since the course of empire to the Indian nations did not run through it.

The early settlers had a hard life in the wilderness of the Pee Dee. The diaries kept by Evan Pugh (1729-1801) are evidence of the struggle to survive and make the land productive through farming (chiefly flax and indigo) and raising cattle.

Isolation of the Pee Dee region was further intensified by its political position in the colony. After the establishment of the Anglican Church in 1707, elections were held at the parish churches, and the church wardens were the election commissioners of the parish. They also had the responsibility of supervising upkeep of roads in their parish and care of the poor. Until 1757 the area in which the city of Florence was later developed was part of Prince Frederick's Parish. The parish church, located on the Black River about 19 miles north of Georgetown, was some 53 miles distant from the site of Florence. In 1757 St. Mark's Parish was created, which, in effect, divided the upper Pee Dee (the "up country") from the lower Pee Dee, but the parish church was located at Pine Tree Hill (later Camden, South Carolina), 45 miles from the site of Florence.

The southeastern Indian Village "Secota." Engraving by Theodore de Bry, circa 1590.

Further exacerbating the plight of the back country was the fact that all of the courts met in Charles Town. If a person in the Florence area wished to vote, he would have to make a journey of over 45 miles each way to the parish church. If he wished to bring a civil suit or make a criminal charge against someone, he would have to travel over 120

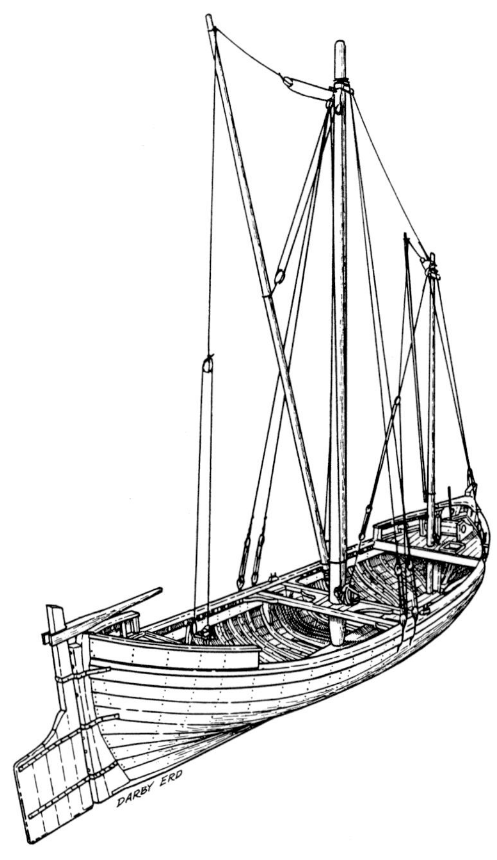

Reconstruction of a trading vessel found at Brown's Ferry on the Black River. These boats were used to trade with settlers who moved into the back country in the mid-1700s. Some features of this reconstruction are now known to be inaccurate for the period. ***Courtesy South Carolina Institute of Archaeology and Anthropology.***

miles to Charles Town to do so. It was a joke among the inhabitants of the back country that they could not answer calls of nature unless they went to Charles Town.

Resentment against the establishment in Charles Town led to what was known as the Regulator Movement. This was essentially a vigilante movement in which the exasperated settlers in the Pee Dee, realizing that their grievances were not going to be redressed in Charles Town, began taking the law into their own hands. One notable incident of defiance of colonial authority took place in what is now Florence County. A constable and a posse of 13 men tried to seize property of some Regulators on the Pee Dee River. Gideon Gibson, a local leader of the Regulators, led a group into a confrontation with the posse. In the ensuing gun battle, one member of the posse was killed, and several of the Regulators were wounded.

This agitation led, eventually, to the creation of Saint David's Parish in 1768, with the parish church located in Cheraw, and the enactment of the Circuit Court Act of 1769, with a courthouse located at Long Bluff near what was later named Society Hill. Saint David's Parish, as an election district, and the Cheraws District, as a judicial unit, were coterminous. The result of these changes put the parish church within 40 miles of the site of Florence, and courts of general jurisdiction within 25 miles.

The first Court of Common Pleas and General Sessions in the Pee Dee met at the courthouse at Long Bluff in September, 1772. On November 19, 1774, nearly two years before the signing of the Declaration of Independence, a presentment was made by the grand jury which emphatically stated the intention of the local inhabitants to defend their right to oppose taxation without representation even "at the hazard of their lives and fortunes." There remained in the area a minority who opposed rebellion. These Tories were relatively quiet during the opening years of the war, but when Charles Town fell to the British forces in 1780, they became more active. The result was a partisan war in the Pee Dee which was destructive of both life and property. One of the Tory leaders, Colonel Fanning, marched from Kingstree to Long Bluff in 1780, burning every meeting house (including Hopewell Presbyterian Church near the location of Florence) and every dwelling of suspected Patriots or their sympathizers in a 75-mile strip. In Long Bluff he hanged Adam Cussack, resident of the Florence area, on the charge that he had fired at the servant of a Tory sympathizer. Atrocities were committed by each side until the surrender and withdrawal of the British in 1783.

In August, 1780, the American Army under General Gates was defeated by General Cornwallis at the Battle of Camden. All organized American resistance to the British occupation within the state ceased. Francis Marion (1732-95) was dispatched to the Pee Dee to organize what eventually became a guerilla war against the occupying British forces. He met with the Williamsburg militia and others, and through bold surprise attacks and quick withdrawals into the swamps of the Pee Dee, he was able to wreak havoc on the enemy. His elusive and cunning tactics earned him the name of "Swamp Fox." His main headquarters was on Snow's Island in what is now Florence County. Marion was a man of limited education but of unquestioned personal integrity. He was fondly remembered by his contemporaries as a leader who, in time of crisis, brought out the best in them. Next to General George Washington, more towns, counties, and institutions (including Francis Marion University) in America are named for him than for any other officer in the American Revolution.

In the decade following the war, the political and social organization of the Pee Dee began to change. The County Court Act of 1785 divided the Cheraws District into three counties: Chesterfield, Marlboro, and Darlington. The act gave the commissioners the authority to locate a courthouse and jail in the most convenient part of each county. The town of Darlington became the county seat for Darlington County, an area which included the site of the future city of Florence. The Long Bluff Courthouse was abandoned, and the county courthouse was established in a new town named Darlington. The South Carolina Constitution of 1790 confirmed the boundaries of the counties, but changed their names to districts.

With the invention of the cotton gin by Eli Whitney in 1793, the vacant land in the Pee Dee could be profitably cultivated to produce a fiber that was in great demand on the international market, particularly in Great Britain. There was a curious contradiction in what transpired. The Industrial Revolution had produced the machinery which made possible the expanded manufacture of cotton fabric, which made cotton production of upland cotton profitable, but which made the use of slave labor an essential part of that expansion in the South. Progress was inexorably ensnared in the greatest of social evils, chattel slavery.

The planters who opened up the lands of the Pee Dee for the raising of cotton were, in most cases, only one generation removed from frontier life.

Southeastern Indian chief.
Watercolor by John White in 1585.

The plantation system provided a comfortable means of making a living, but it was no sinecure. It required hard work and attention if it was to succeed.

There were three large plantations which covered most of the land on which the village of Florence would be developed. These were owned by Thomas McCall Jr. (1800-1844), who owned almost 1,000 acres and 12 slaves; James A. Pettigrew (1800-1879), who owned over 2,000 acres; and Hugh Muldrow Jr. (1784-1843), who owned over 2,000 acres and 17 slaves. Two of the original plantation houses from the Pettigrew plantation still stand in the present city of Florence.

In the Pee Dee, the opening of new lands for cotton farming led to a realization that the transportation system used to get the cotton produced to the port city of Charleston was inadequate. The use of the Pee Dee River for this purpose was dependent on the rise and fall of the river level, and roads were not dependable because there was no reliable program for keeping them in usable condition. This situation led to a further contradiction. In order to improve the means of transporting cotton to the available market, the building of railroads, linchpin of the Industrial Revolution, would be necessary.

***Right:* Colonel Francis Marion prevents the lynching of a Tory leader, Captain Butler, who surrendered himself to Marion at the conclusion of the Revolutionary War in 1782. The scene, painted by William deHartburn Washington in 1858, is set at Burch's Mill in what is now Florence County. The original painting hangs in the lobby of the State House in Columbia.**

Cotton cultivation became economically feasible with the invention of the cotton gin by Eli Whitney. Watercolor by Jane Jackson.

ATLANTIC COAST LINE
1031
FREEMAN HOUSE
1856 - 1870
WILMINGTON COLUMBIA & AUGUSTA
CHERAW & DARLINGTON
NORTHEASTERN, AND ATLANTIC
COAST LINE RAILROAD STATIONS
1874 - 1908

Chapter Two

Building the Railroads

(1847-60)

Marker at the location of Freeman House, built in 1856. Locomotive 1031 was placed at the site but later removed. ***Photograph courtesy of Howard Waddell.***

Charleston, formerly the chief supplier of South Carolina's cotton to European markets, suffered a dramatic economic decline in the period from 1819 to 1825. The need to boost these export revenues led to efforts to make Charleston more accessible to planters in the midlands and upcountry. But even a state-financed program to improve roads and build canals failed to produce the desired boost in Charleston's economy. Charleston then turned to the building of a new industrial development, railroads.

The South Carolina Canal and Rail Road Company built, in 1830, a 135-mile railroad from Charleston to Hamburg on the South Carolina side of the Savannah River opposite Augusta. However, the state of Georgia refused to allow a trestle to be built over the river, fearing that Georgia-grown cotton would then be diverted from Savannah to Charleston. The South Carolina Rail Road then built a line from Branchville, South Carolina, to Columbia, South Carolina, in 1842, and from Kingsville, South Carolina, to Camden, South Carolina, in 1848. None of these lines penetrated the Pee Dee region.

However, a third depressed port city entered the struggle in 1846. Wilmington, North Carolina, seeking to divert cotton from Charleston, sponsored the incorporation of a railroad which would extend from that city across the Pee Dee region and make juncture with the South Carolina Rail Road's Camden Branch line at the town of Manchester in Sumter District. It was necessary for the Wilmington and Manchester Rail Road to be incorporated in both North Carolina and South Carolina, which was accomplished by January 9, 1847. The charter stated the railroad would be built from Wilmington to a point within 10 miles

Illustration of a locomotive, circa 1850

General W.W. Harllee

of the village of Darlington "thence by the most practicable route to or near Manchester, in Sumter District… ." This "point" would become the first station, named Florence.

The railroad company was organized, and in June, 1848, the stockholders elected the Governor of North Carolina, E. B. Dudley, president. Dudley was succeeded by William Wallace Harllee (1828-97), who served from 1848 until 1855. President Harllee, a native of Marion District, became an energetic and ardent promoter of the railroad, whose construction was commenced in 1848.

The method of raising the funds for the construction presented another contradiction. The landowners through whose lands the railroad was to pass were asked to enter into a contract by which the slaves on the plantation would be the labor force for the clearing and grading of the right-of-way, and the plantation owners would be paid with shares of stock in the railroad. Again, the institution of chattel slavery was being used to promote an industrial revolution in the South.

The building of the Wilmington and Manchester Rail Road through the woods and fields of the Pee Dee area inevitably led to new crossings which had the potential of becoming villages. One of these was the crossing of what

William Wallace Harllee
(1812-97)

General W.W. Harllee is the most distinguished native of the Pee Dee region whose name is connected with the early history of the city of Florence. He promoted the building of the Wilmington and Manchester Rail Road in the 1840s and 1850s and served as its president at the time it was constructed through the area now occupied by the city of Florence. Harllee was born near Little Rock in Marion District, was admitted to the South Carolina Bar in 1834, and practiced law in Marion. In 1885 he was named president of the newly formed South Carolina Bar Association. In 1889 General Harllee moved to Florence to live and practice law.

His military career in the militia began when he was elected a major in 1837. Harllee was promoted to colonel and led an expedition of South Carolina militiamen to Florida to fight the Seminole Indians. In 1845 he was promoted to the rank of brigadier general and became a major general in the militia in 1861.

Harllee was elected to the South Carolina House of Representatives from Marion District and served from 1836 to 1838, and from 1846 to 1848. In 1860 General Harllee was elected lieutenant governor and served on Governor Pickens' executive council from 1860 until 1862. He was also a signer of the Ordinance of Secession.

During the early days of the Civil War, General Harllee was ordered to have the militia build a fortification on the Pee Dee River near Bostic in what is now Florence County. "Fort Finger," as it was called, was erected to prevent Federal gunboats from coming up the Pee Dee River and destroying the Wilmington and Manchester's bridge over the river. He never held a commission in the Confederate Army, but later in the war he raised a group of militia known as the "Pee Dee Legion," which was stationed near the coast.

Harllee served as the presiding officer of the Democratic convention which nominated Wade Hampton for governor in 1876. He was elected to the South Carolina Senate from Marion County, 1880-84, and served as president *pro tempore* of the state's senate, 1882-84. In the heated election of 1890, General Harllee was a leader in the movement opposing Tillman. He never took a prominent part in politics after Tillman's election. He died in 1897. His daughter, Florence Henning Harllee (1848-1927), continued to live in Florence and taught school there.

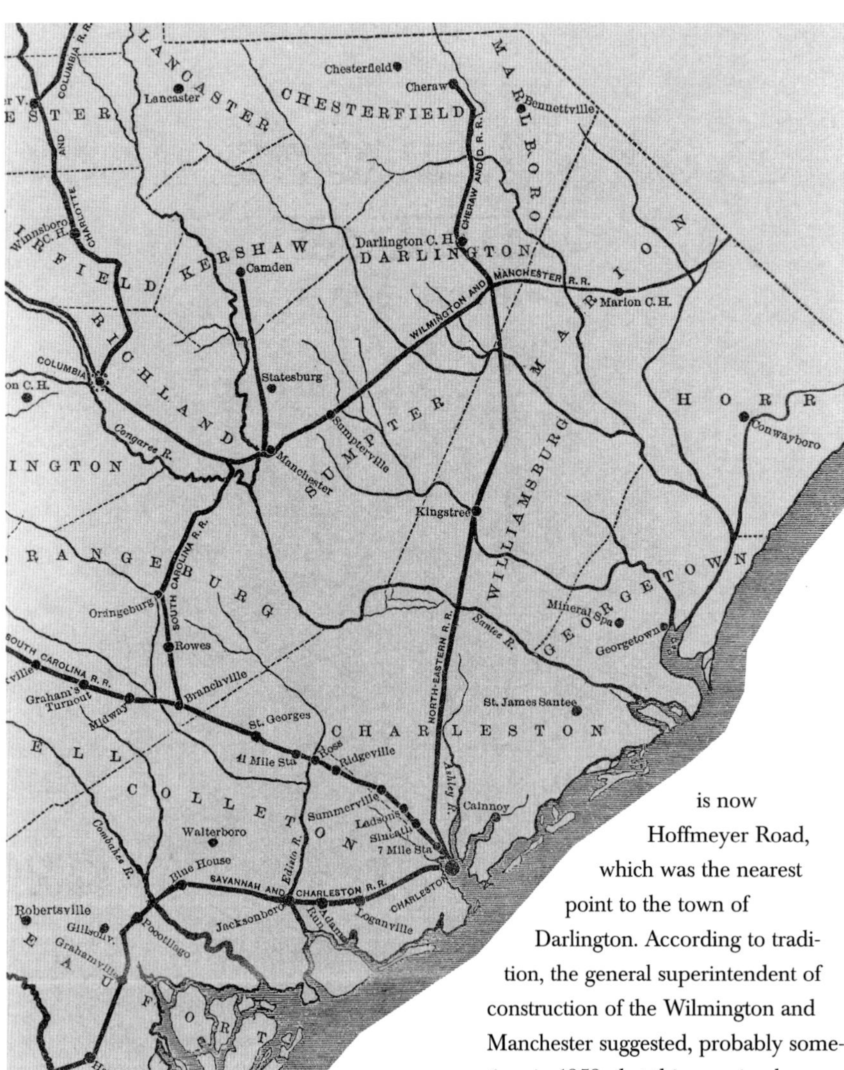

Map showing the railroads which existed in South Carolina in 1860

is now Hoffmeyer Road, which was the nearest point to the town of Darlington. According to tradition, the general superintendent of construction of the Wilmington and Manchester suggested, probably sometime in 1852, that this crossing be named Harlleeville in honor of the company's president. That name presented difficulties, as there was already a Hardeeville and a Harleyville in the state. It was then decided to name the crossing for the president's daughter, Florence Henning Harllee. She was named for a character in Charles Dickens' *Dombey and Son,* the novel her father was reading at the time of her birth in 1848.

In 1853 the Wilmington and Manchester Rail Road purchased five acres of land from John T. James "for a depot nearest Darlington Court House called Florence." It was to be used for a depot, toll house, water station, engine shed, wood sheds, workshops "or other buildings for the necessary accommodation of the said company." Judge Joshua H. Hudson, a recent graduate of South Carolina College, recalled that on January 7, 1853, he traveled from Columbia by rail "to Kingsville, thence to Florence, then existing only in name, as the only structure was a pine board shed all else [being] a pine forest."

The Wilmington and Manchester's bridge over the Great Pee Dee River was completed in October, 1856, forging a link in a line of railroads which would eventually connect Montgomery, Alabama, with New York. Granted, the route was circuitous and fragmented by separate corporations which owned the various links in the chain, but it was a new and revolutionary transportation system which, in the prophetic words of the promoters, followed the "Atlantic Coast."

It was apparent from the outset that if the railroad linking the Pee Dee basin of South Carolina to Wilmington was to be successful, there would have to be one or more feeder lines both north and south of the Wilmington and Manchester's tracks in South Carolina to reach deeper into the Pee Dee. The area north of the Wilmington and Manchester line, including Darlington, Chesterfield, and Marlboro Districts, was receptive to the idea of a branch line.

In 1849, while the Wilmington and Manchester was under construction, the South Carolina legislature chartered the Cheraw and Darlington Rail Road. The act incorporating the Cheraw and Darlington Rail Road had provided simply that it was authorized to construct a railroad "from the Town of Cheraw to some point on the Wilmington and Manchester Rail Road, in the District of Darlington, by a route to be determined by the company... ."

A typical train of the 1850s

By 1851 Charlestonians began to react to the threat which the Wilmington and Manchester posed. The act of the legislature chartering the North Eastern Rail Road provided that it was authorized to construct a railroad "from the City of Charleston to such point on or near the Wilmington and Manchester Rail Road, West of the Great Pee Dee, as may be selected… ." The North Eastern Rail Road and the city of Charleston offered to subscribe to $100,000 of Cheraw and Darlington stock if it would build its line to link up with the North Eastern. In addition, the North Eastern agreed to commit to at least $25,000 a year in transportation over the Cheraw and Darlington's line. In December, 1852, the South Carolina Legislature authorized the state to subscribe to $100,000 worth of Cheraw and Darlington's stock, but only on condition that the Cheraw and Darlington connected its line with the North Eastern's line. The short 40-mile railroad which had experienced difficulty in raising capital was now in business, and the Wilmington and Manchester was thwarted in trying to divert cotton from the Pee Dee region to Wilmington.

The Cheraw and Darlington, after striking a deal with the North Eastern, began construction in 1854, and the line from Cheraw to the Wilmington and Manchester was completed on December 19, 1855. However, the intersection was not made at the crossing called Florence, but at McCown's Crossing, some two miles to the east where Church Street crossed the present railroad tracks in the city of Florence.

A hotel called the "Freeman House" was built almost immediately at the intersection. It was later referred to as the "Old Hotel." One early Florence citizen, reminiscing about her childhood, described the platform of the depot as being "covered with turpentine barrels…a famous place to play hide and seek."

The abundant pine forests in the area provided a natural resource which was readily exploited for turpentine, lumber, cross-ties, and firewood. There is evidence that a sawmill existed once at the northeastern corner of what later would become Evans and Dargan Streets. Its location there probably accounts for the misalignment of East and West Evans Streets.

Alfred Ford Ravenel
(1822-93)

Alfred Ford Ravenel was born in Charleston, South Carolina, December 22, 1822. Although he never lived in Florence, he and his family's business had a profound influence on its creation, development, and economic growth. A graduate of the College of Charleston, he was elected president of the North Eastern Rail Road in 1857 when he was only 35 years old, and served as its president until his death in 1893. The Ravenel family played a major role in the early development of railroads in South Carolina, in the development of Florence as a municipality, and for bringing this railroad through the difficult period following the Civil War. John Ravenel, the father of Alfred, served as president of the Cheraw and Darlington Rail Road in 1871-72 and 1887-92.

The Ravenel firms began as importers of woolen cloth from Rhode Island and England and served as cotton factors for the producers of raw cotton in the state and exporting the cotton abroad. At one time the firm had seven vessels, all full square-rigged ships. These ships went regularly from Charleston to European ports carrying cotton, naval stores, and rice and returning with a variety of cargo. Ravenel saw the North Eastern Rail Road and Florence as an extension of that international trading system.

The North Eastern Rail Road, however, had grander plans for a town. In March, 1854, the North Eastern Rail Road purchased 577.6 acres of land from the estate of Thomas McCall. This purchase would determine the location of the future city of Florence. But the name Florence did not attach to the new location immediately. On April 1, 1854, the directors of the North Eastern passed a resolution as follows: "Resolved, that the Station at the Junction of the North Eastern Rail Road and Cheraw and Darlington Rail Road be called Wilds, in complement [sic] to the late Judge Wilds of this State." Judge Samuel Wilds (1775-1811) was the late father-in-law of the president of the Cheraw and Darlington Rail Road. On December 11, 1855, however, the minutes book of the North Eastern shows that an agreement had been reached between that company, the Cheraw and Darlington, and the Wilmington and Manchester Rail Roads that a joint depot would be built with each company sharing one-third of the cost. It is probable that at this time the decision was made to abandon the name Wilds, which the North Eastern had selected, and move the name Florence to the new location. Undoubtedly, "Florence," which literally means "city of flowers," is a better name for a city than "Wilds." Perhaps the directors of the three railroads feared that the name Wilds would become descriptive rather than denominative.

According to all reports, the Cheraw and Darlington operated efficiently and profitably. Its success was largely attributable to its first presidents before 1860, Dr. Thomas Smith (1793-1875) and Allan McFarlan (1819-69). Both men had been born in Great Britain and achieved notable successes in this country.

Pettigrew plantation home in what is now the city of Florence. Built in 1850, it is currently owned by Mr. and Mrs. Mark Buyck Jr. *Photograph courtesy of Mark Buyck Jr.*

Construction on the North Eastern line began in January, 1853, using white labor. As in the case of the Wilmington and Manchester, the white workers proved unreliable, refusing at times to work at all. Once again, slave labor was used to construct the line. Progress was steady and the line was opened to Florence on October 5, 1857.

The North Eastern, under the guidance of its president, Alfred Ford Ravenel (1822-93), recognized the potential of the 577.6 acres it owned. The company directed that streets and lots be laid out for the town's growth. Seven streets are shown on the plat of S. S. Solomons, drawn between 1858 and 1860. The street names reflect pride in local jurists and celebrities. Three are named for judges (Evans, Dargan, and Cheves); three are named for prominent citizens chiefly from the upper Pee Dee (Coit, Irby, and McQueen); and one, Front Street (now Baroody Street), for its location. The plat shows a joint freight depot between Irby and Coit Streets and a passenger shed across from Gamble's Hotel. The hotel, completed in 1860, was built by the North Eastern for the convenience of travelers and to promote the sale of lots in Florence. In 1862 it was sold to Joseph W. Gamble (1804-89). From 1860, until it burned in 1893, Gamble's Hotel was the social and political center of the town. This handsome two-story building seemed to bring a touch of the charm and elegance of Charleston into the back country.

The introduction of steam engines and rolling stock as part of the railroad system created feelings of awe and affection toward these symbols of the industrial age. The locomotives particularly were thought of and called "iron horses," that being the closest analogy in the natural world for these instruments of power and usefulness.

Like their farm animals and pets, they were given names which bespeak

Gamble's Hotel, built by the North Eastern Rail Road in 1860, was the center of activity in the village of Florence for over 30 years. Watercolor by Jane Jackson.

both admiration and affection. These included names of famous persons, presidents of the railroads, parishes, and general names like "Mercury" and "Courier." Oral tradition has preserved the account of the first arrival of the freight engine named "Florence" in the village. It seems that some romantic or sentimental employee of the North Eastern, in honor of the occasion, painted on the side of the engine the face of a young girl with golden curls.

By 1860 the Wilmington and Manchester had 20 locomotives. Eleven of these were passenger locomotives, seven were freight, and two were called gravel locomotives. The Cheraw and Darlington had only three, and the North Eastern had thirteen locomotives. These machines were the lifeblood of the infant village, and were thus treated, at the start, with affection. But possibly an awareness of inevitability of the impersonal and dehumanizing nature of the tools of industry is reflected in the fact that when the 19th engine was purchased by the Wilmington and Manchester just before the Civil War, it was simply designated "Number 19."

Chapter Three

Florence and the Civil War

(1860-65)

A typical scene of a train during the Civil War. It was not unusual to have Confederate soldiers standing guard duty at important locations. The equipment and rolling stock of the North Eastern Rail Road which was sent from Charleston to Florence was guarded by Confederate soldiers. *Reprinted by permission of Toof Engraving Co., Memphis, Tennessee.*

From a previous state of isolation, the village of Florence would suddenly be thrust into the mainstream of events by the outbreak of war in 1861. In 1860 the village consisted of approximately 100 residents. There were two clusters of buildings in the village. In the east was the second depot, the Freeman House, the Jacobi House, and the Presbyterian Church, which was built in 1860. A pine forest separated them from the western group consisting of Gamble's Hotel, a ticket office, a bar, a drug store, and several other store buildings.

An illustration of Federal troops in Cheraw, South Carolina, in March 1865. Saint David's Church is pictured in the background.

The war literally passed through Florence on the railroads. The great and near great of the Confederacy and Union armies, traveling from and to Richmond, Charleston, and Savannah, detrained at Florence and availed themselves of the hospitality of Gamble's Hotel. Conspicuous among them was General Robert E. Lee, who, traveling north by train in 1862 to take command of the Army of Northern Virginia, passed through Florence accompanied by his horse, "Traveller," and the diarist Mary Boykin Chestnut, who records that in passing through Florence her husband attempted to get a cup of coffee, and the train pulled out without him. After the war, General U. S. Grant changed trains in Florence on his way to Charleston. A resident of that period recalled: "[E]very now and then the few citizens here saw something of the struggle in the long trains of box cars loaded with soldiers, packed inside and on top, and maybe a flat car or two loaded with cannon passing through here going from one point to another where an attack was expected. Occasionally a car passed draped in mourning, bearing some officer who had fallen in battle." Wounded and sick Confederate soldiers passing through Florence occasioned one of the first civic ventures in the village. Some 62 workers, mostly women from the surrounding area, established a soldiers' wayside home in the two-story wooden structure known as the Norris Building. The building became known as the "Wayside Hospital," and its work was carried on, initially, by voluntary donations of money, time, and produce. In the latter part of 1862, or the first part of 1863, the number of sick and wounded became so great that the Confederate government took over the operation, and Dr. Theodore Dargan, of Darlington, was made physician in charge. He was assisted by a matron and corps of nurses and servants and the women of the community, who continued to visit the hospital and give voluntary aid. The office of the doctors assigned to the hospital was located across the railroad tracks facing Gamble's Hotel. Approximately 64 soldiers died there during the course of the war and were buried in the graveyard of the Presbyterian Church on Church Street.

The bombardment of Charleston by Federal forces brought streams of refugees into the midlands. Cottages were built in the woods and roads were opened which, in time, developed into streets. One of these refugees was Mrs. Frances Church, who was characterized by a contemporary as "a woman of remarkable character and force" and "indefatigable in all good works." Mrs. Church came with her brother, Job Dawson, and his family. She, with two other refugees from Charleston, Miss Samuella Phillips and a Miss Colby, opened a school. This was not the first school, however, in what is now

Florence. Before the arrival of Mrs. Church, there had been a school known as "Florence School" conducted by Miss Henrietta Hunter in 1856, and later, one conducted by Tom Cook from Bennettsville in a small schoolhouse west of the Jacobi House on Front Street.

The naval blockade of the Confederacy closed down ports like Charleston, Wilmington, and Savannah, except for blockade runners. The attempt to build warships to help break the blockade led to the decision to move some of the main Confederate shipworks inland, to the relative safety of the banks of rivers like the Pee Dee. In 1862 the Confederate government authorized the construction of a navy yard on the east bank of the Pee Dee River in Marion District, some 14 miles from Florence. The site proposed for the naval yard was just north of the Wilmington and Manchester Rail Road's crossing on the Pee Dee River, which meant supplies could be brought in easily by rail.

Construction of the CSS *Pedee* at Mars Bluff Navy Yard began almost immediately. The navy yard was surrounded by an embankment on which were mounted at least two 24-pound Howitzer mortars to defend the yard and trestle against any upriver attack. Within the yard were some 14 buildings and an excavated dry dock in which the CSS *Pedee* was built.

General W. W. Harllee, commander of the "Home Guards" in the Pee Dee area, aided the Navy Yard's officers in securing workmen and supplies. The construction of the gunboat became something of a community project. The ladies on nearby plantations offered to sell their jewelry to help pay for the ship they called their "boat."

The gunboat is described as a ship of the "Macon Class": 150 feet long with a 25-foot beam, and a draft of 10 feet. She was schooner-rigged as well as fitted with steam-driven double propellers (a recent innovation), thus making her a versatile craft. Under steam, the *Pedee* could make nine knots. The armaments on the CSS *Pedee* consisted of three pivoting guns: two Brooke

The First Presbyterian Church, built in 1860, was the first church built in Florence. *Photograph courtesy of the First Presbyterian Church.*

One of the propellers of the CSS *Pedee* salvaged in 1928. *Photograph by Kris Trahnstrom.*

Rifles (rifled cannon), a 6.4-inch and a 7-inch, one at bow and one at stern, and a 9-inch Dalghren amidships. The CSS *Pedee* was launched in January, 1865, with a public celebration. The state's governor was on hand, as well as other dignitaries and crowds from around the area. Because of Sherman's rapid advance into South Carolina, orders were received to take the ship upstream to Cheraw to cover the retreating Confederate army. Upon completion of this assignment, the *Pedee* returned to the Navy Yard and there the decision was made to scuttle the *Pedee* to keep her from falling into enemy hands. Accordingly, each of the *Pedee's* three cannons were fired into the swamp, removed from their mounts, spiked, and thrown into the river at the ship's mooring. An augur hole was bored into the *Pedee's* hull, which was loaded with powder, and sometime between March 15 and 18, 1865, the CSS *Pedee* was set on fire and pushed out into the river. After she drifted over a quarter of a mile downstream, she was blown apart and sank.

Eventually, in September of 1925, the remains of the hull, boilers, and propellers of the *Pedee* were exposed when a long drought lowered the level of the river. The twin propellers of the ship were salvaged and brought to Florence, where they are now on the grounds of the Florence Museum. The three cannons have never been recovered.

When General William T. Sherman advanced into Georgia in the summer of 1864, a problem was created for the Confederate government with regard to Union prisoners. There were two large prisons in Georgia: Macon and Andersonville. To prevent the prisoners' being freed by Sherman, they were moved across the state to Charleston, South Carolina. Charleston, however, was under siege from Federal forces on land and sea. Moreover, the Federal prisoners brought disease with them which could only worsen Charleston's situation. Thus, in September, 1864, they were ordered removed by rail to Florence, where a new Confederate prison stockade was under construction.

In October, 1864, the first prisoners arrived, by rail, at the Florence Stockade, which was located about one mile southeast of Florence and was constructed using slave labor from local plantations. The stockade consisted of a 1,400-by-725-foot palisade supported by a five-foot earthen embankment made from dirt taken from a seven-foot deep trench that ran around the outside of the palisade to prevent tunneling. At each corner of the palisade stood a raised platform upon which an artillery piece was mounted. The interior of the stockade was divided by a small stream providing both fresh water and a means by which to dispose of waste.

A report on the prison at Florence, dated October 20, 1864, showed 12,362 prisoners in the stockade and 807 Federal soldiers, who had taken the oath of allegiance to the Confederate government, living outside its walls. Conditions inside the stockade were so appallingly bad that in about five months, 2,738 prisoners died and were buried on land furnished by Dr. James H. Jarrot, now the National Cemetery.

In February, 1865, Sherman's army reached Columbia, necessitating a speedy removal of the prisoners from Florence. A general exchange, however, was offered by the Federal authorities on February 17, 1865, and the prisoners from the Florence stockade were ordered to be shipped out sometime after February 24, 1865. Approximately 6,500 able-bodied prisoners left Florence for Cheraw on March 5, from whence they were marched to Wilmington for exchange.

On February 1, 1865, Sherman marched into South Carolina with an army of over 65,000 men and approximately 20,000 camp followers. Opposing him was a Confederate force of fewer than 30,000. The Union Army was divided into two wings, and Sherman skillfully misled the Confederates into believing that Charleston was his primary target. Much equipment was sent inland from Charleston to keep it out of Sherman's incendiary reach. There was surprise and dismay when he turned toward Columbia and marched across the midlands of the state.

The village of Florence, while not a major objective of Sherman's wrath, became a lesser target. After burning Columbia during the night of February 17 and into the next morning, Sherman proceeded toward Camden and Cheraw. The Confederate authorities decided to evacuate Charleston, to withdraw all Confederate troops from the coastal area, and to rush them by train to Cheraw to confront the Federal forces advancing toward North Carolina. The North Eastern Rail Road was used to transport about 30,000 men with equipment, guns, and ammunition to Florence. The rolling stock of the Wilmington and Manchester and a small amount belonging to the Cheraw and Darlington were used to transport the troops from Florence to Cheraw. The Confederates, however, decided to retreat to Fayetteville, North Carolina, and large quantities of powder and guns were captured in unloaded cars left by the Confederates in Cheraw. In addition, Sherman's forces captured and destroyed one of the Cheraw and Darlington's locomotives.

The Federal army at Cheraw set about to destroy all rail, rolling stock, depots, and trestlework of the area's other railroads. Part of this destructive operation, ordered shortly after Sherman's troops entered Cheraw, was an expedition to Florence to destroy the railroad and station there and the trestlework between Society Hill and Florence. The Federal troops of 546 men left Cheraw on the morning of March 4 and moved to within seven miles of Darlington, to camp for the night. On the morning of the fifth, the Federal troops proceeded to Darlington, destroying all trestlework, burning the Darlington depot and 250 bales of cotton. They then proceeded toward Florence to destroy the depot, the railroad locomotives, and the rolling stock.

General Robert E. Lee on his horse "Traveller." Both Lee and his horse changed trains at Gamble's Hotel during the Civil War.

At the crossing of Ebenezer Road and the Cheraw and Darlington railroad, a train was sighted moving toward Darlington. The advance units immediately deployed on both sides of the track to capture it. The engineer, however, saw the Federal troops waiting in ambush, threw the locomotive in reverse, and began racing backward toward Florence at full throttle. The mounted Federal troops followed in hot pursuit. Fortunately for the Confederates, a detachment of cavalry was at the Florence depot awaiting orders. Though their horses were still in rail cars, the Confederate cavalrymen, notified of the attack, were able to rush out to oppose the Federals. A skirmish erupted just west of the depot and eventually moved to the very center of the village. Some of the attacking Federal troops reached the depot building, but were unable to either hold it or set it on fire, and the Confederates drove the Federals back. Upon receiving word that 400 additional Confederate troops with artillery were coming by train from Kingsville, the Federals retreated. The Confederate forces pursued the retreating Federals and engaged their rear guard, forcing them to retreat to Society Hill. The Federal report showed seven wounded and eight missing, but no record exists of the Confederate losses.

The destruction of the North Eastern's locomotives and rolling stock, concealed on a siding in Florence, was prevented when Federal troops were driven back. The Wilmington and Manchester and the South Carolina Rail Road's locomotives and rolling stock had been sent to Sumter and Camden to prevent their destruction, which remained a prime military objective of the Federals.

Beaufort, Charleston, Georgetown, and Wilmington were, by the end of February, 1865, in Federal hands. On April 5, 1865, Brigadier General Edward E. Potter, commanding a Federal force of approximately 2,700 men, marched from Georgetown, South Carolina, to Sumter for the purpose of destroying the locomotives and rolling stock between Camden and Florence. On April 9, at Dingle's Mill near Sumter, a Confederate force of approximately 700 to 800 (mostly young boys and old men) engaged the Union troops. In that futile battle, one of the last in South Carolina, 26 Federal and approximately 50 Confederate soldiers died. The Federal juggernaut occupied Sumter that same day, ironically, the day on which Lee surrendered to Grant.

In Sumter, the Federal forces destroyed 4 locomotives, 8 cars, a carpenter shop, car and blacksmith shops,

Drawing of the destruction of a locomotive by Federal troops

a freight depot, storehouses, and a million feet of lumber. They also destroyed a locomotive, railroad buildings, and a small train of cars at Manchester. At the Wateree junction a detachment destroyed 8 locomotives and 40 cars and 3 miles of trestlework over the Wateree Swamp. On April 19 and 20, at Middleton Depot, the Federal forces destroyed 18 locomotives and 176 cars mostly filled with ordnance stores, railway machinery, and naval and quartermaster's stores.

Potter moved his command to Georgetown on learning of Johnston's surrender to Sherman on April 21, and could boast the destruction of 32 locomotives and 250 railroad cars. The Wilmington and Manchester lost virtually all of its equipment, and the track from Camden to Florence was destroyed. It had taken nine years to build the Wilmington and Manchester Rail Road and only three days to destroy it.

The three railroads in the Pee Dee, however, were able to resume operations quickly. Where the trestles had been destroyed, ferries were used to take the locomotives and cars across the rivers until the bridges could be rebuilt. By July 1, 1865, the North Eastern commenced operations; by July 10, 1865, the Cheraw and Darlington was back in operation. By August 25, 1865, the Wilmington and Manchester, whose construction marked the beginning of the history of the city of Florence, was back in operation, but it had to borrow $2 million it could never repay.

Drawing of the burial of Federal soldiers who died in the stockade and were buried on land of Dr. James H. Jarrott. The burial ground later became a national cemetery.

Chapter Four

Recovery, Reconstruction and Incorporation

(1866-76)

Railroad depot, circa 1876.
Photograph courtesy of Dr. G. Wayne King

Confederate veterans were attracted to Florence after the Civil War. Jerome P. Chase (1838-1919) made such a conspicuous contribution to the growth of the village that his obituary referred to him as the "Father of Florence." James Allen (1832-1913) walked from Greensboro, North Carolina, to Florence, spent the night on the porch of Gamble's Hotel, and remained to become a successful merchant and civic leader. William Alexander Brunson (1837-1911) left Wofford College to join the Confederate Army, was severely injured in the battle of Seven Pines, taught school briefly, engaged in the newspaper business, and became an attorney in Florence.

Along with the Confederate veterans came carpetbaggers, non-Southerners seeking personal gain from the radical Republican government. Benjamin Franklin Whittemore (1824-94), the quintessential carpetbagger, was prominent in the Florence area from 1865 to 1877. A native of Massachusetts and chaplain in the Union army, Whittemore held important political offices and influenced the development of Florence. Among other charges made against him, Whittemore was expelled from the United States House of Representatives for selling appointments to West Point. Not all carpetbaggers, however, were as controversial as Whittemore; some became pillars of the community.

Troops of the 167th New York Infantry arrived in Florence by train in June, 1865, as part of the army of occupation. The officers and Freedman's Bureau officials took rooms in Gamble's Hotel. The enlisted men pitched tents in the pine woods between Coit and Irby Streets. Aside from preventing the outbreak of further hostilities, the main

---

From *South Carolina During Reconstruction* by Francis Butler Simkins and Robert Hilliard Woody. ©1932 by the University of North Carolina Press. Used by permission of the publisher.

duty of the troops in Florence was to reintegrate former "rebels" into the new American society. Essential to this process was the administration of an oath of allegiance to the United States to all former Confederate soldiers and citizens.

A critical responsibility of the occupying Federal officers was to review and approve contracts between planters and their former slaves. When complaints were made, noncommissioned officers were generally sent to investigate. If there was a serious controversy, formal proceedings would be instituted through the commissioned officers who, acting as provost marshals, served as judges in criminal proceedings.

All was not grim oppression and hostility with the Federal army of occupation. It was reported that "There were tournaments at Darlington, and tournaments at Florence, at which queens of love and beauty were crowned; and officers of the garrisons seemed to enjoy these occasions."

In response to the problem of integrating the recently freed slaves into the community, the Federal government also set up the Bureau of Refugees, Freedmen, and Abandoned Lands (commonly called the Freedman's Bureau) to help feed, clothe, house, and educate freed blacks as well as white refugees. The blacks used the benches in front of Gamble's Hotel as a meeting place.

Nine new stores were built in Florence in 1869, doubling the merchant population. In addition to the North Eastern Rail Road's shops, there were eleven stores, three hotels, a restaurant, a bar, a millinery shop, a brickyard, two drug stores operated by doctors, a carriage shop, three churches, and numerous residences. A newspaper article published that year notes that the merchants in Florence were, in effect, acting as factors in helping planters sell their cotton: "It is usually true that many of the planters did better this season [1868] in selling their cotton to the Florence merchants than shipping to Charleston or Wilmington, and the amount of this staple bought at Florence this season is more than three times as much as any previous year."

Florence was one of the commercial towns that developed in South Carolina during Reconstruction. The country store owners and town merchants would "furnish" merchandise, food, and equipment, to be paid for, with interest, when the crop was sold. Increasingly, suspicion arose on the part of the rural white farmers that these merchants and bankers were scheming to cheat them of their profits. Merchants in Florence were not immune from this distrust.

One of the ill effects of Reconstruction was the type of leaders it produced. In the period immediately following 1865, there was hope that the new social order would bring new economic opportunities. When this did not happen, the leaders of the postwar period were shorn of their romantic optimism. The Reconstruction experience caused many white Southerners to become "frugal, cautious, and practical." This was increasingly true of merchants in Florence, offset, to some extent, by the railroads, which sustained optimism and economic growth.

In 1867 the North Eastern's repair shops were relocated to Florence. The railroad's locomotives, rolling stock, and portable machinery had been successfully hidden there. The advent of the North Eastern's shops brought jobs and an influx of inhabitants. Approximately 200 people were employed by the railroad in 1870. These employees and their families constituted more than half of the village's population. Among the new citizens coming to Florence to work for the North Eastern was Daniel W. Haines (1841-91), a Confederate veteran and master railroad mechanic.

A watercolor by W.S. Dowis Jr., representative of a dwelling house built in Florence in the 1870s

By July 19, 1866, the *National Baptist,* a periodical published in Philadelphia, reported, "At the close of a protracted meeting in Florence nineteen hopeful converts were buried with Christ in Baptism." Shortly thereafter, the congregation, led by the Reverend D. M. Breaker, built a small wooden church on the southeast corner of Irby and New (Palmetto) Streets. The site proved eminently suitable, for immediately behind it was a pond which was used to baptize a growing congregation.

The Central Methodist Episcopal Church began meetings in the home of M. C. Henry in 1867. It was organized as a congregation with 17 members in 1870, and the first church building was constructed that year at the northeast corner of Dargan and Cheves Streets, but before completion, it was destroyed by a cyclone. A second building, which served the Methodist congregation during the early years, was constructed on the same site.

The Episcopal congregation, consisting of only a dozen families, had begun meeting in Freeman's Hotel in 1865. It had been unusually large during the Civil War years because of refugees from the low country, and a wooden church at the southwest corner of Darlington and Coit Streets was completed in 1867.

The development of black churches in the village of Florence followed the sectarian lines established by the leading Christian denominations. The Methodist Church was a leader in the prewar years to convert slaves to Christianity, and other denominations encouraged church attendance either in their slave galleries, a standard feature of most antebellum churches, or through special services conducted after the white congregation had finished worshiping. Former slaves lost no time in forming churches modeled after the white denominations, with one notable difference. The black churches became centers for political discussion.

Cumberland Methodist Episcopal Church traces its origins to 1865, when a group of approximately 16 people began meeting in the home of Joseph and Sarah Kershaw near Evans Street. As the congregation grew, it moved out of the house and into the yard. In May, 1866, the Missionary Society of the Methodist Episcopal Church bought a lot on Coit Street, which is part of the present site of Cumberland Methodist Church. Among the trustees who were the grantees in the deed were B. F. Whittemore and Joshua E. Wilson (1844-1915), a prominent member of

Joshua E. Wilson
(1844-1915)

Joshua E. Wilson was born in Charleston in 1844 and was probably one of that small group of blacks who were emancipated before the Civil War. He was educated by a private tutor and studied for the ministry. In 1868 Wilson was placed on a trial basis to stations in the Centenary Church in Charleston, the Kingstree Church in Kingstree, and Cumberland Methodist Church in Florence by the conference of the Methodist Episcopal Church. In December, 1871, he was ordained by the bishop.

Mr. Wilson was active in the public school which was built in Florence in 1868, and after its first principal, Thomas C. Cox, was elected sheriff of Darlington County, became the principal, and served in that position for several years.

The Reverend Mr. Wilson was first elected to the town council of Florence in April, 1874. He served as a warden on the town council at least through the year 1879. He served as postmaster for Florence on four separate occasions: February, 1876-April, 1883; January, 1885-March 1886; May, 1890-May, 1894; and July 18, 1899-September, 1909. During the period of his public service, no one seriously questioned his ability or his integrity. In the Methodist Church, he was appointed presiding elder over several districts in South Carolina, including the Florence District, which was created in 1882. He died on November 21, 1915.

the church, and later a Methodist minister and member of the town council of Florence.

Trinity Baptist Church traces its origins to a small prayer group organized in 1867 under the leadership of the Reverend Wesley J. Parnell. The congregation met on Front Street in the home of a member known as Mother Lindsey. In 1868, on a site near the corner of Marlboro and Dargan Streets, under a makeshift shelter, Trinity Baptist Church was organized. One of its deacons at that time was N. D. Harper, who was elected a warden when Florence was incorporated.

A uniform system of free public schools was created for the first time by the 1868 state constitution. The first public schoolhouse in Florence, built on the southwestern corner of Dargan and Palmetto Streets on land now part of the Poynor School property, was known as the "Blue School," apparently because of its color. Later, it became known as Wilson School, probably named for Henry Wilson, congressman from Massachusetts, later vice president under Grant. The first teacher was T. C. Cox, a black man who belonged to that small group who were free before the Civil War. He was considered an intelligent and able man who had also been elected sheriff of Darlington County. He was succeeded by Joshua E. Wilson. The school was attended almost entirely by black children; the white children attended private schools. Wilson School continued in operation on Dargan Street until 1906, when it was torn down to make way for Central School (later Poynor). The present Wilson High School is its direct successor.

In the latter part of the 1860s, events were taking place outside of South Carolina which were to have far-reaching consequences for the village's future. The North Eastern and the Cheraw and Darlington Rail Roads had been slowly recovering from the devastation of the Civil War. The Wilmington and Manchester Rail Road, however, could not meet its payments on its two-million-dollar debt.

In September, 1868, a syndicate called the "Southern Railroad Project" was formed in Baltimore, Maryland, for the purpose of acquiring the Wilmington and Manchester Rail Road. Their objective was to control a series of railroads, from Richmond, Virginia, extending southward through Charleston to Savannah. It was the beginning of what would eventually become the Atlantic Coast Line Railroad. The syndicate purchased the Wilmington and Manchester's outstanding debt and most of its stock in April, 1870, naming their new corporation the Wilmington, Columbia and Augusta Railroad.

With the Wilmington and Manchester in its possession, the syndicate turned their attention toward acquiring other railroads, including the North Eastern and the Cheraw and Darlington Rail Roads, which resisted absorption for years. The company eventually ran its tracks across the Wateree River from Sumter to Columbia, bypassing the town of Manchester in Sumter County. The new railroad's reach was toward Atlanta, Georgia, not Charleston.

Newspapers were a part of the development of Florence from its beginnings. In 1866 the *Florence Gazette* made its appearance as a weekly. It was described by a contemporary as "a small but neat

From *South Carolina During Reconstruction* by Francis Butler Simkins and Robert Hilliard Woody. ©1932 by the University of North Carolina Press. Used by permission of the publisher.

Drawing of emancipated slaves voting for the first time in 1868. Reprinted from Trawbridge, *A Picture of the Desolate State.*

sheet." There was no printing press in Florence; therefore, the paper was printed on the press of the *Southerner* in Darlington. S. A. Brown (1837-1923) was the publisher, and Jerome P. Chase and W. A. Brunson were the editors. Both Chase and Brunson were active in the newspaper business for the next 20 years. Chase was also the editor of a paper in Darlington known as the *Darlington Democrat* published by Edward Lucas. When Lucas died in 1871, the *Democrat* died with him. B. F. Whittemore published a radical Republican newspaper in Darlington called the *New Era.*

In 1872 W. Wallace McDiarmid, a North Carolinian, established the *Florence Pioneer,* which lasted for a little over a year. The Florentines gave the *Pioneer* the humorous name of "The Bugle Horn of Liberty." The *Pioneer* appears to have been a controversial newspaper. The *Charleston Daily News* reported on January 7, 1873: "The *Florence Pioneer* complains of a Ku Klux Klan attack on their office on Thursday night [January 2, 1873] last, and calls upon Governor Moses for protection. The editor, however, seems to have been able to take care of himself, as he slammed the door of his office into the faces of the desperadoes, and was not at all alarmed when they endeavored to blow up the establishment with a teaspoon of gunpowder." When McDiarmid left, Chase and Gamble bought the *Pioneer* and owned it jointly for a number of years. Eventually, Chase bought Gamble's interest and published it alone.

By 1870 the village of Florence had an estimated population of 700. On January 13, 1871, State Senator Benjamin F. Whittemore introduced a bill in the legislature to incorporate the town of Florence. The members of the House of Representatives from Darlington County, all black, supported this bill, which became law on March 9, 1871.

The town's corporate limits were determined by a circle whose center was to be the southwest corner of Dargan and Front Streets and whose radius was one mile. This circle enclosed what would become the city of Florence until the first annexation in 1948.

The town council was made up of an intendant (mayor) and four wardens (councilmen) elected for one-year terms. Curiously, the act provided that if any person, upon being elected intendant or warden, refused to act as such, he was required to forfeit $20 to the town council "for the use of said town." The town council was to pass ordinances "respecting the roads, streets, market and police of said town, as shall appear to them necessary and requisite for the security, welfare, and convenience of said town, or for preserving health, order, peace and good government within the same... ."

The most controversial provision of the act was the council's authority to grant or refuse licenses "to keep taverns, or retail spirituous liquors within the corporate limits of said town... ." Once granted, these licenses could not extend beyond the term of office of the council granting them. This was of vital concern to the future prosperity of the numerous saloon keepers.

The police force consisted of two or more marshals and the Darlington County sheriff, who also served as town marshall. Council was given the right to construct a "guard house" and to commit, for not more than 24 hours, any person who, within the corporate limits of the town, "may be engaged in disorderly conduct, open obscenity, public drunkenness, or in any conduct grossly indecent or dangerous to the citizens of the town... ."

A board of health was established, and property owners were required to keep the streets in front of their lots "clear of all filth and rubbish, and also to make and keep in good repair sidewalks in front of said lots when the same shall front on or adjoin any of the public streets of the said Town... ." Each male citizen was required to donate one day's service annually to clean the city's streets.

Jerome Chase was elected intendant on April 10, 1871. Elected as wardens were Aaron Weinberg, Chesley D. Bristow, Plato C. Fludd, and N. D. Harper. Bristow (1841-1919), a Confederate veteran and native of Marlboro County, was one of the first inhabitants of the crossroads which became Florence. Aaron Weinberg, a Jewish merchant from Charleston, opened one of the first stores in Florence. Fludd was an ex-slave from Charleston who was appointed magistrate in 1870 and later elected treasurer of Darlington County. Nathanael D. Harper, an educated ex-slave, was one of the founders of Trinity Baptist Church in Florence and served as town clerk from 1871 to 1874.

The second intendant of the town, John Kuker (1845-1926), was Jewish. Kuker had been born in Hamburg, Germany, became a pharmacist, and, after immigrating to the United States in 1865, was employed by McKesson & Robbins in New York. He moved to

The railroad shops of the Wilmington, Columbia and Augusta Railroad in 1879

Florence in 1866, opened a mercantile establishment, and became a successful merchant and moneylender. In addition to serving as intendant, he was also elected warden (1876-78 and 1884-86).

Jerome P. Chase

In April, 1874, the town elected Daniel W. Haines as intendant and J. E. Schouboe, Arthur Moisson, T. L. Bennett, and J. E. Wilson as wardens. The first three elections set a precedent; two white wardens and two black wardens were elected. This continued until the election of 1876, and thereafter, one black warden was elected until the election of 1896.

Haines was faced with two different opponents in the elections of 1875 and 1876. In the April 12, 1875, election he defeated Fludd, one of the original wardens. In the deceptively calm election held on April 10, 1876, Haines, identified with the railroad interest, defeated W. J. Norris (1831-1907), a business partner of Jerome Chase. The four wardens elected were Kuker, J. E. Schouboe (1853-1913), Wilson (black), and Albert Baruch, a Jew, former magistrate of Florence, and radical Republican.

The wasteful spending and corruption of the radical Republican legislature caused taxes to rise to an unbearable level. In the summer of 1876, General W. W. Harllee, as well as William Little, editor of the *Florence Pioneer,* made speeches to a political gathering in Layton's Hall at which time they voiced their uncompromising support of white Democratic candidates over the predominantly black Republicans. This came to be known as "the straight-out movement." The *Florence Times* declared its motto, "red hot and straight-out."

The state's Democratic party convened in Columbia in August, 1876. General W. W. Harllee, a known "straight-out" advocate, was elected president of the state convention, which nominated General Wade Hampton for governor. Hampton declared, "By the Eternal! I will be governor of South Carolina." He succeeded, but not without a bitter struggle.

In the general election of November, 1876, control of state government was at stake. Senator Whittemore was holding over, since he had been elected to a four-year term in 1874. The four incumbent Republican candidates for the House of Representatives in Darlington County were black, while the Democratic party's nominees were all white. Democrats were alarmed by a report that on election day Senator Whittemore had been urging blacks to set fire to the fields adjacent to Florence to distract and intimidate white voters. Violence and election fraud on both sides were a possibility, so United States Army soldiers encamped on Front Street, ostensibly to see that the election was conducted fairly.

Florence, the largest polling place in the area, became the focus of the political struggle. Democratic headquarters was set up in Layton's Hall at the corner of Evans and Dargan Streets, while the Republicans occupied a store on North Dargan Street. The town became a cauldron of political ferment. Militant white Democrats, or "Red Shirts," were treading a thin line between an outward show of physical force and the danger of precipitating violence that could bring the intervention of federal troops.

The Red Shirts, primarily Confederate veterans, organized as a pseudo-military organization in support of white Democrats. Its distinctive uniform was a red shirt. To counteract the Red Shirts, the Republicans relied chiefly on its militia units, which were predominantly black.

Both organizations began activities early on election morning. The first to the polling place were some white Democratic voters, escorted by Red Shirts. The black Republicans followed, marching in columns of two and singing "Hold the Fort, for I am Coming." There were three election managers on duty that morning, one white, and two black, with a black supervisor. The voting had already commenced when the supervisor arrived, demanding that the managers open the ballot boxes. They refused and when the supervisor became "too boisterous and pertinacious," one white poll-watcher knocked him down. Federal troops were called in, but made no arrests. At one point, when the number of whites at the polling place had diminished, the Timmonsville Red Shirts were brought in on a train to boost morale. At the end of the day, the Republican candidates had won a majority vote for all offices in Darlington County. The white

Jerome P. Chase
(1838-1919)

Jerome P. Chase was born in New Market, Tennessee, but when he was three years old his family moved to Laurens, South Carolina, and some years later, to Washington, D. C. The greater part of his education was received in Washington. As a young man he worked as clerk in the offices of Congressman Justin S. Morrill, Congressman John C. Breckinridge, later vice president, and Congressman James L. Orr of South Carolina.

Chase volunteered for duty in the Confederate Army, and as a telegraph operator, became acquainted with the village of Florence. After the war, he returned to Florence, opened a store, and, within two years, became a realtor and insurance broker, his chief business interests until his death. He was, however, a versatile entrepreneur and was either president, director, or organizer of early newspapers, the first ice factory, the first electric light plant, and of many other businesses.

Chase was elected the first chairman of the board of selectmen of the village, and after the incorporation of the village as the town of Florence in 1871, he was elected the first intendant of the town. In 1878, he was elected to the General Assembly of South Carolina as a representative from Darlington County, but did not run for reelection. However, when a vacancy occurred in 1881, he was elected to fill that unexpired term. An effective supporter of education, he served frequently as a school commissioner.

Jerome Chase was an active and influential member of the executive committee which was formed to push the legislation through the assembly to create Florence County. The town became the city of Florence in 1890, and Chase was elected the first mayor. As a sign of respect when he died, all of the stores and businesses in Florence closed during the funeral service.

Democratic voters were not deterred, however, in their efforts to upset the election returns. The election results in South Carolina became the center of a national debate, the resolution of which would determine the next president of the United States.

The difficulty was that both Democrats and Republicans claimed victory in local and statewide offices. The Republican, Governor Chamberlain, was sworn in on December 7, and one week later, the Democrat, General Hampton, was sworn in as governor. There were two state Houses of Representatives–the Wallace House (consisting of 65 white Democrats), and the Mackey House (consisting of 59 predominantly black Republicans).

On the local level, two magistrates were appointed in Florence. Republican Governor Chamberlain's appointee was L. W. Williams, a black man who had been elected chief marshal (police chief) by the town council in April, 1876, and Democratic Governor Hampton appointed W. A. Brunson. For a period of time there were dual and rival courts, each claiming exclusive jurisdiction.

During the period of uncertainty following the elections, the level of violence rose in the Florence area. Unsavory characters who often follow in the wake of social turmoil drifted into the new town. A gang of outlaws

A contemporary drawing of former black slaves holding a political rally. Reprinted from Trawbridge, *A Picture of the Desolate State.*

known as the "Manning Gang" was particularly active at this time, attacking homes in the rural areas, burning barns, and stealing livestock. They spent much of their time in north Florence and in the woods west and northwest of the town.

Front Street and the streets extending from it must have looked very much like a western frontier town with saloons, wooden store buildings, boardwalks connecting the main business establishments, and unpaved streets that were alternately dust bowls and quagmires. And like a frontier town, Florence had many of its vices–public drunkenness, prostitution, and violence.

It was in this context of unrest that the Guard House Riot took place on March 13, 1877. The town authorities had arrested a black man. An angry crowd gathered outside and began clamoring for his release, causing a white posse to be summoned to defend the guard house. Governor Hampton wired the town authorities that he wanted no incident which would involve federal troops. In the initial stages of the riot, black women threw bricks at the white men guarding the jail. One member of the posse had two of his front teeth knocked out by a brick hurled by the protesters, but the matter did not end there. About 100 black militia came into town, went into the guard house, removed the prisoner to the outskirts of town, and released him. Most of the blame for the riot and the actions of the black militia was attributed to Senator Whittemore.

On April 10, 1877, as part of the compromise in the Hayes-Tilden presidential election, federal troops were withdrawn from South Carolina after 12 years of occupation. D. W. Chamberlain, B. F. Whittemore, and many other leading Republican families in the Florence area fled the state.

The town of Florence had acquired such a reputation that it was reported to be "the rendezvous of the most notorious rogues and murderers in the state." Governor Hampton used the state constabulary in an attempt to break up the outlaws in Florence and sent three "detectives" (today's SLED agents) to assist the magistrate, to no avail. The governor then sent the chief of the state's constabulary, who stated "that unless the condition of things improved [he] would bring down the constabulary and sweep the town clean." ❧

Three Grand C
Entertainme

AT GAMBLE'S H

Florence, S. C.

October 23d, 24th and 25th

FOR THE BENEFIT OF THE LADIES MEMORIAL A
THE FLORENCE LIBRARY ASSOCIAT

Wednesday Eveni

These Entertainments will commence with the very amusing a
comedy entitled "*Everybody's Friend.*" The cast of characters
sure the utmost success. All the well known and fovorite Ama

Thursday Evenir

Grand Instrumental and Vocal CONCERT for which occasion
talent *from abroad* has been secured.

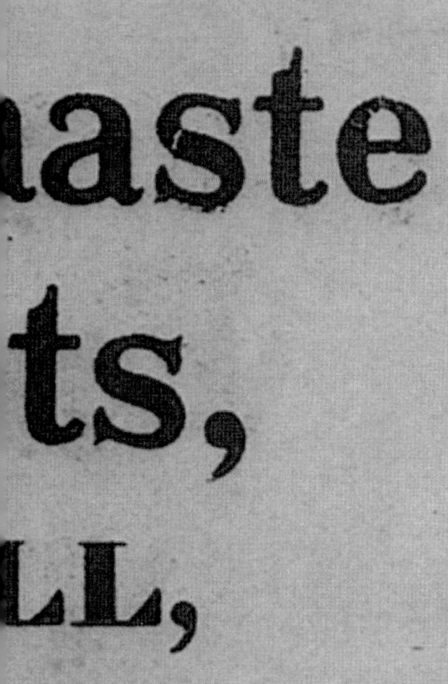

aste
ts,
LL,
1878,
OCIATION AND

interesting three act
ll be such as to in-
rs will take part.

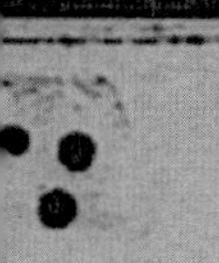

very best amateur

Chapter Five

A Town Becomes a County Seat

(1877-88)

An 1878 playbill from the collection of the Darlington County Historical Commission

Florence Rifles, circa 1880.
Photograph courtesy of Dr. G. Wayne King.

In the wake of the 1876 election, there was a burst of activity in the formation of civic organizations in Florence. These were roughly of three types: utilitarian, sentimental, and cultural. In the first category, the two most prominent were the voluntary fire companies and the paramilitary association. The Rainey Hook and Ladder Company, chartered in 1874 to honor black Congressman Joseph H. Rainey, was made up of predominantly black members. The Hope Steam Fire Engine Company was chartered in December, 1882, and had as its motto "We hope to save." Both companies provided municipal services the town could not afford. They raised the money to purchase fire equipment and served as volunteer firemen. The Florence Rifles, similar to a national guard unit, was chartered in February, 1878, and was available to supplement the police force in times of widespread public disorder.

The second type of organization represented a sentimental, or fraternal, manifestation of civic activity. A group of predominantly female citizens, outspoken in their loyalty to the memory of the Confederacy, organized in 1878 the Florence Memorial Association to raise funds for a monument at the graves of Confederate soldiers buried at the Presbyterian Church. A monument was ordered and dedicated in 1882. When the church was sold, the remains of the Confederate soldiers and the monument were moved to Mount Hope Cemetery in 1905.

The drab, small-town existence created a hunger for both the exotic ceremony of Masonic orders and the comradeship of fraternal societies. The Ancient Free Masons, Hampton Lodge No. 204 organized in 1879; Knights of Pythias; Harmony Lodge, No. 8; Knights of Honor Florence Council, No. 916; American Legion of Honor; Chosen Friends; and Golden Chain were some of these. The fraternal spirit was extended beyond this life when a Fraternal Burying Ground was created at the end of East Pine Street.

The growing cultural interest was evidenced by the organization of a library association in 1878 by Belton O'Neall Townsend (1855-1981). The library was operated out of his law office and by 1883, had acquired 1,800 volumes, a figure which compared favorably with the 2,000 volumes credited to Winyah Indigo Society of Georgetown in 1876. Only the Charleston Library Society (15,000 volumes) and two Due West library societies (2,500 volumes) ranked appreciably ahead of Florence.

To raise money, the library association engaged in several fund-raising projects. In October, 1878, it sponsored with the Ladies' Memorial Association "Three Grand Chaste Entertainments" at Gamble's Hotel, including a three-act comedy entitled *Everybody's Friend,* promising "all the well known and favorite amateurs" and that for the second night's instrumental and vocal presentation, "the very best amateur talent from abroad has been secured." The finale to this series was a "silhouette performance" and dance. In addition, *East Lynne* and *HMS Pinafore* were performed to raise money for the library.

Separation of the races in the school system started early in Florence. In 1873 the Florence Education Association was chartered by the legislature, and a school for white children was constructed on the east side of Irby Street between Cheves and Palmetto Streets.

In 1883 the South Carolina General Assembly created a separate public school district for Florence. Although the statute creating the school district provided for a tax levy for support, the schools were not free. The school board was allowed to charge, in addition to taxes, an assessment on each scholar "as supplementary tuition fees." One by one the private schools closed, and the town's school district, reinforced by teachers from the private schools, began operating *de facto* segregated schools.

Anti-Catholicism and anti-Semitism, which flourished elsewhere after Reconstruction, were absent in Florence. In fact, from the very beginning of Reconstruction, both Jews and Roman Catholics were not only accepted, but they were also active politically, and frequently elected to office.

The Roman Catholic Church got its start in 1863, when John Joseph Moisson, a gunsmith by trade, came to Florence as a refugee from Charleston. The first Mass in Florence was celebrated in his home. The congregation continued to meet in the homes of members until 1886, when it was financially able to build a wooden church at the northeast corner of Palmetto and Irby Streets.

Citizens pose with a locomotive in the 1890s. *Photograph courtesy of Howard Waddell.*

From the beginning, the Jewish population of Florence was influential in business and civic affairs. Like the Roman Catholics, they had a strong base of support in Charleston, where Jewish families had formed a congregation in 1749. Moritz Jacobi, who built the Jacobi House, came to America from Denmark and, in 1857, settled in the village of Florence. During Reconstruction, most of the Jews in Florence supported the Democrats, with the notable exception of Albert Baruch. Baruch operated a store on Front Street, was appointed a magistrate, served on the town council, and was elected sheriff of Darlington County. He was generally mistrusted, and after the Democrats came to power, he disappeared.

Two outstanding Jewish citizens of the 1880s were David Sternberger, a merchant, and Isaac Sulzbacher (1884-1920), a jeweler. Both were members of the executive committee formed to promote the creation of Florence County. Sternberger was born in Bavaria, became a citizen of the United States, and, in 1872, moved to Florence and opened a store. He was one of the organizers, in 1882, of the Hebrew Benevolent Association, which had for its purpose "creating and maintaining an Israelite's burial ground, and for education and religious purposes." It was largely due to this organization that the congregation known as Beth Israel was incorporated in 1912.

In 1877 the North Eastern Rail Road closed its shops in Florence. For 10 critical years the shops

Thomas Wilson Talbot
(1849-92)

A native of Chesterfield, Thomas Wilson Talbot began working in a shoe factory when he was 10 years old to support his widowed mother. After the Civil War, he apprenticed himself in the North Eastern Rail Road shops, and when he had completed his apprenticeship, he was an engineer on that railroad until 1874. When the North Eastern closed its shops, Talbot, like many other employees, transferred to the new shops operated by the Wilmington, Columbia, and Augusta Railroad in Florence. He ran into difficulty with management, however, when he successfully organized nine fellow machinists to form the first union of machinist and mechanical engineers in this country.

Talbot was discharged in 1887 by the Wilmington, Columbia, and Augusta Railroad as a result of his unwelcome organizing activity. Undaunted, he sought employment with another railroad and, in 1888, organized the first lodge of what became the Order of United Machinists and Mechanical Engineers of America. He returned to Florence and formed the second lodge. By 1890 there were 101 lodges in the United States. He served as a warden of the town of Florence (1882-83) and as a member of the initial executive committee (1887) to promote the new county.

Talbot died as a result of a gunshot wound. The accused, two brothers from a prominent Florence family, were tried for murder and acquitted. Years later, one of them was elected mayor. In 1948 the Machinists' Union erected a statue of Talbot in Grant Park in Atlanta. His grave, originally in the Fraternal Cemetery, was moved to Mount Hope Cemetery in Florence and is marked by a 10-foot monument, placed there by the Machinists' Union.

had not only provided employment opportunities, but had also nurtured political and civic leaders of the growing town. The decision to close the shops coincided with the Wilmington, Columbia, and Augusta Railroad's decision to build its shops and new passenger station in Florence.

The new depot was built on the site of the Freeman House, at the southeastern corner of Front and Church Streets. The shops were built across the tracks facing the depot. In order to connect the new depot, the North Eastern Rail Road constructed a curve in its tracks turning away from the depot on Coit and Front Streets. The effect of the changed location on the growing town was far-reaching. The North Eastern Rail Road had endeavored to channel the development of Florence to its land south and west of Gamble's Hotel. Now the direction of development for the next 50 years would be eastward, and the surrounding residential development would become known as East Florence.

The expanding activity of the railroad shops after 1877 produced a middle class and new folk heroes in Florence. The officials of the railroads (principally the Wilmington, Columbia, and Augusta Railroad), the master mechanics in the railroad shops, the engineers, and the conductors gave the town's social and political life its distinctive character.

From management came William H. Day (1842-1928), a Confederate veteran who came to Florence as "Master Car Builder" employed by the North Eastern Rail Road Company. When the North Eastern closed its shops, Day was employed by the Wilmington, Columbia, and Augusta Railroad in the same capacity. He served as warden from 1878 to 1880, and as intendant in the years 1883-84 and 1888-90. When

Saint John's Episcopal Church, 1889. It is the oldest church building which has been in continuous use in Florence. ***Photograph courtesy of Dr. G. Wayne King.***

the town was incorporated, he was elected mayor twice, serving in that office for the terms 1895-97 and 1897-99.

It was the engineers, however, who excited the most admiration among the public. The town kept up with the speed records of the local engineers and their locomotives with the same zeal as sports fans memorizing their favorite team's scores. There were engineers who had reputations both for caution and fast running, and the death of any of these in a train wreck occasioned citywide mourning.

If engineers were admired for their heroics, conductors were respected for their stable, middle-class virtues. Before the Civil War, many sons of local plantation owners became conductors. They were given the honorary title of "Capt'n," frequently held municipal offices, and demonstrated a devotion to civic duties and hard work. While the town remained small, there was a family feeling among the railroad men evidenced by the fact that their unions were officially named "Brotherhoods." Thomas Wilson Talbot (1849-92), former employee of the North Eastern, brought another contradiction to the town of Florence–a trade union. In 1888 he organized the first lodge of what became the Order of United Machinists and Mechanical Engineers of America.

One problem that haunted both the Wilmington and Manchester and its successor, the Wilmington, Columbia, and Augusta Railroad, was the loss of time involved because the route from Florence to Richmond, Virginia, required stopping first in Wilmington. The solution became known as the "Wilson Shortcut"– that is, a railroad from Florence directly north to Wilson, bypassing Wilmington. It was promoted by the North Eastern, and financial interests in Charleston. The Florence Railroad Company was chartered in 1882 to build a line from Florence directly into North Carolina, but was not completed until 1891. Alfred F. Ravenel, president of the North Eastern Rail Road, was one of its incorporators.

The 1880 census showed a population of 1,914 in the town of Florence, evidence of its extraordinary growth. While the largest employers in the town were the three railroads, the town's merchants also provided employment and constituted a separate political grouping whose interests were frequently at odds with the railroad's. The first division in town elections was between the Republicans (predominantly black) and the Democrats (predominantly white). The election of W. J. Norris, who defeated Intendant D. W. Haines in 1877, represented a triumph of the merchants over the railroad interests. W. A. Brunson, an attorney, replaced Norris in the election of 1879, but, in 1882, Z. T. Kershaw, a machinist and locomotive engineer, became intendant. In the 1879 election, the ultraconservatism of some of the officials surfaced in the debate on whether or not to build a town hall. One warden "suggested that it would be proper to submit the question to the Tax Payers of the

Town for their approval or objection to the building of a Hall." In 1883, however, a town hall and market were constructed without submitting the proposal to the taxpayers.

The municipal election of 1883 was pivotal in the movement to create a new county with the town of Florence as the county seat. Pitted against each other were two of the town's leaders: Captain W. H. Day and Belton O'Neall Townsend. Townsend was only 28 years old, and too young to have served in the Confederate Army. He launched his campaign for intendant with a broadside printed as "Supplement to the *Florence Times*" dated March 13, 1883. In the statement of his candidacy, Townsend started the fight which led to the formation of a new county. He declared that Florence was destined to become a county seat, and, if elected, he promised to "inaugurate, agitate, and vigorously push upon the people of the region interested and the Legislature the measure to cut out a new county from Marion, Darlington, and Williamsburg, with Florence for the county seat."

Not content with promoting the idea in the local municipal election, Townsend fired broadsides into Marion, Darlington, and Kingstree. He stated, with some exaggeration, "Florence now has 3,000 inhabitants–more than all the other towns and court houses on this [the 4th] Judicial Circuit put together. Yet we are forced to hunt for and [if found] resort to obscure villages at a distance, [which have missed their legitimate province as good cotton fields] to record our liens, mortgages, titles and bills of sale." He pointed out that Marion County was divided into East and West Marion by the Pee Dee River, a natural barrier which sometimes prevented access to the courthouse.

Townsend was defeated by Day, but the significance of the political campaign transcended his defeat. For the first time, there was a clear articulation of what the ideal town of Florence should be. Also, for the first time, there was a cogent statement of the arguments in favor of making Florence a county seat. True to the campaign promises made during the election, Townsend became the principal promoter and propagandist of the new county movement.

In November, 1886, the movement to create the county of Florence was organized. A mass meeting of the citizens of Florence and surrounding areas was held at Allen's Hall to discuss the subject of petitioning the legislature at its approaching session. An executive committee was elected "to urge a new county." The committee was composed of 27 members from the west portion of Marion County and 20 members from Darlington County. The assembled citizens elected Dr. James Evans chairman of the committee, and Townsend, secretary.

Townsend composed a six-page pamphlet entitled "Why The Proposed NEW COUNTY of Florence

ACL baseball team, circa 1900. ***Photograph courtesy of Dr. G. Wayne King.***

Dr. James Evans
(1831-1909)

James Evans was born in Marion and attended the Citadel, graduating in 1853. He was employed as a civil engineer by the North Eastern Rail Road to make the survey for its tracks which eventually determined the site of the town of Florence.

He was next employed in building the New Orleans and Mississippi Railway and, 1857, was placed in charge of building levees along the Mississippi and Arkansas Rivers, where he contracted malaria and yellow fever. His health was so impaired that he gave up engineering and sought another profession.

In 1859 Evans enrolled at the University of Pennsylvania, and received a medical degree in 1861. With the outbreak of the Civil War, he volunteered for service in the Confederate Army, was appointed a regimental surgeon, and saw duty throughout the war in Virginia.

After the war he settled in the Mars Bluff area of Marion County. In 1877, however, he moved his family to the rapidly growing town of Florence and remained a resident there until his death.

Both Evans and his wife were active in civic affairs. In the newly formed Florence Library Association, Evans was president, and his wife was secretary. When the move to create Florence County became an organized public effort, he was chosen as chairman of the executive committee to organize and promote that project. He was the central figure around whom diverse interests and supporters rallied.

His service to Florence as its chief physician brought recognition to him both in the state and nation. He was elected president of the South Carolina Medical Association in 1890, and in 1895 was appointed by the governor to the State Board of Health, and served as its administrative officer. His work in the area of sanitation and containment of infectious diseases led him to publish papers on typhoid fever, diphtheria, consumption, and cholera. He received a bronze medal at the Paris Exposition in 1900 for his work in the area of public health in South Carolina.

His daughter, Jane B. Evans (1866-1950), became the founder of the Florence Museum.

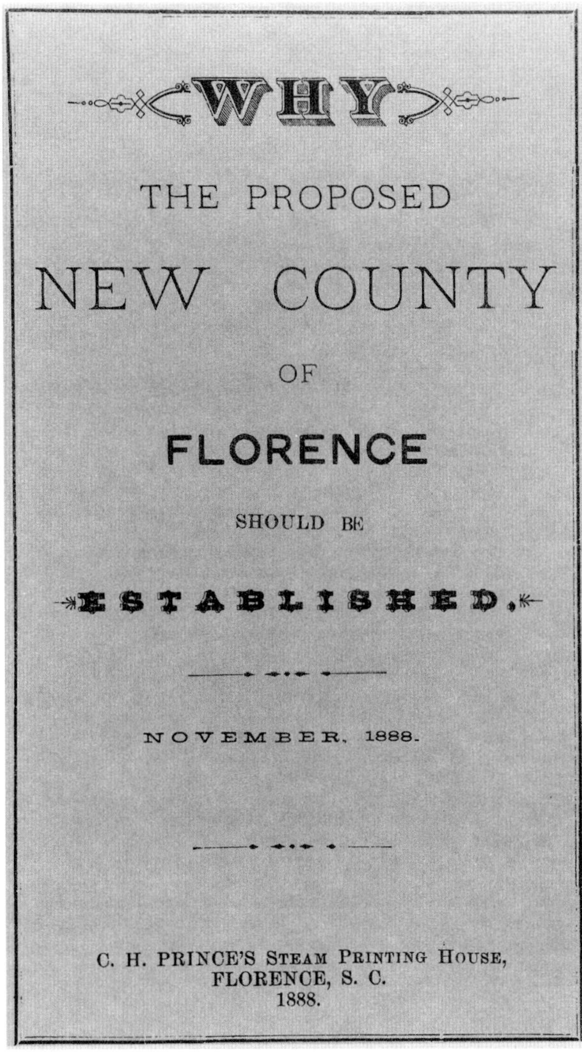
WHY
THE PROPOSED
NEW COUNTY
OF
FLORENCE
SHOULD BE
ESTABLISHED.

NOVEMBER, 1888.

C. H. PRINCE'S STEAM PRINTING HOUSE,
FLORENCE, S. C.
1888.

Pamphlet advocating the creation of Florence County

Should Be Established." It was published in 1887, and republished in 1888 in an expanded version. The pamphlet stated that, "The Town of Florence by votes [unanimous] of a taxpayers' meeting, and of its Town Council, has pledged itself to provide the jail and court house, free of expense to the new county, and at the cost of the town, provided they be located in Florence... ."

The Darlington News wasted no time in disparaging the effort to create a new county from the southern portion of Darlington County. In the December 9, 1886, issue, it made the following sneering observations:

"Our sister town of Florence has made more effort to make something of herself than any town in the State; and has in a measure succeeded. She had a most unpromising location in the low flat woods but being a railroad center she has gathered about her an energetic population, who by constant push and enterprise aided by the railroad influence and patronage, have built up a town of considerable pretensions. In her effort to outstrip her neighbors on some occasions she has exhibited a grasping disposition."

The proponents of the new county realized that a broader base of support was needed than the town of Florence. Success would require sufficient statewide support in the legislature. In particular, it meant getting representation on the legislative delegations of Darlington and Marion Counties.

One leader who played a crucial role in securing representatives favorable to the new county was Zachary Taylor Kershaw (1849-1910), a machinist and locomotive engineer who later became an attorney. A native of New Jersey, he settled in Florence in 1878, was elected intendant in 1882, was a trial justice for the next several years, and was elected to the House of Representatives from Darlington County for the term 1886-88.

The election of Kershaw, an active member of the executive committee, to the House of Representatives from Darlington County was viewed as a great advantage to the new county movement. The greatest opposition emanated from the town of Darlington, so having Kershaw as a member of the Darlington County legislative delegation gave the new county proponents a great advantage. There was, however, in the House of Representatives another member of the executive committee promoting the creation of Florence County, Leonard Smiley Bigham (1816-1906). Bigham was elected to the House of Representatives from Marion County in 1886. He was from West Marion and it was generally assumed that the residents of West Marion favored the creation of a new county; therefore, his election did not attract the attention that Kershaw's did. He was constantly at odds with both Marion County's senator and with its other house member. He ran against the incumbent senator in 1888 and was soundly defeated.

On November 23, 1887, Kershaw presented to the House of Representatives a petition with the sig-

Belton O'Neall Townsend
(1855-91)

Born in Bennettsville, South Carolina, Belton O'Neall Townsend attended Saint David's Academy in Society Hill, entered South Carolina College at age 15, and graduated at 18. The only graduate in the class of 1873, young Townsend wrote a series of articles about conditions in South Carolina and the 1876 election, which he sent to William Dean Howells, editor of the *Atlantic Monthly.* They were published in the February, April, and June 1877 issues of that magazine. Another article which he had sent to Howells appeared in the October 14, 1876, issue of the *New York Tribune.* These articles were published anonymously because Townsend's observations were so critical of the attitudes of white southerners that it was considered dangerous to make his identity known.

His father, Benjamin D. Townsend (1815-85), president of the Cheraw and Darlington Railroad, was violently opposed to Townsend's ambition to become a journalist, so he agreed to become a lawyer and write as an avocation. He was admitted to the practice of law and opened an office in the town of Florence in 1878.

Townsend was short in both stature and temper. He had a quick wit and was fond of satire. A political broadside which he wrote during the municipal election in 1879, in rhyming couplets, indicates that he had a deep contempt for the sort of politics being practiced in the town.

He immersed himself in civic activity, serving as librarian of the first library, as an actor in the musicals and plays which were produced to raise money for the Library and Monument Association, as a captain in the Florence Rifles, as organizer and leader of the Hope Fire Company, as a 32nd-degree Mason, and as vestryman in Saint John's Episcopal Church.

He ran unsuccessfully for intendant in 1883, and published a book of poems entitled *Plantation Lays* in 1884. He also published a pamphlet entitled *Why The Proposed NEW COUNTY of Florence Should Be Established*, which contained the strongest and most influential arguments in favor of the formation of Florence County.

He died in a fire which consumed his home in February, 1891. His widow, Leah McClenaghan, remarried and, as Mrs. Daniel M. McEachin (1865-1945), was prominent in civic work after his death.

natures of 333 citizens of Darlington, Marion, and Williamsburg Counties for the creation of the county of Florence, with a surveyor's map of the proposed county attached. A bill to create the county came up for consideration and passed the House of Representatives, and then was sent to the state senate, where it died in the senate committee.

The new county's prospects suffered another blow when Kershaw was defeated in his bid for reelection to the House of Representatives in 1888. There was a compensating gain for the new county movement, however, in the election of Richard Grandison Howard (1832-90) from Marion County to the House of Representatives, replacing Bigham. Howard, a distinguished Confederate veteran, unlike Kershaw, came from the antebellum planter class with a long background of family connections in Marion County. He was so widely respected that, when the act to create the county was passed, there was an effort to name the county "Howard" instead of Florence.

Having failed to secure passage of the new county bill in December, 1887, the executive committee immediately regrouped. A special meeting of the council was held on November 28, 1888, for the purpose of securing funds to pay for the lobbying effort to get the county bill passed. Town council agreed to contribute $100 to aid the executive committee of the new county movement.

The pamphlet published by the executive committee and revised in the fall of 1888 raised the issue that Darlington County was seeking, deliberately, to deprive the growing community of Florence of representation in the state legislature. The strategy which the executive committee developed was to introduce the bill in the House of Representatives and Senate, simultaneously. It was assumed from the voting in the House in the 1887 session that there would be a comfortable margin in favor of the new county when the vote was taken in 1888. The Senate, which defeated the first attempt to create the county in 1887, was perceived to be the most difficult obstacle in 1888.

Marion County's Senator Moody introduced the bill in the Senate, and it passed on December 17, 1888. The Senate bill then went to the House of Representatives, came up for consideration on December 19, 1888, and passed on December 22, 1888. In order to secure the necessary 625 square miles required by the Constitution, Darlington County was to contribute 262 square miles (including the town of Florence); Marion County, 300 square miles; Williamsburg County, 28 square miles; and Clarendon County, 38 square miles. Florence County had come into being, and there was an outburst of rejoicing, for the town was at last a county seat.

Florence Machine Shop, circa 1900. ***Photograph courtesy of Dr. G. Wayne King.***

An affluent Florence couple of the 1880s

GROCERIES

Chapter Six

Growing Pains As a City

(1890-1917)

West Evans Street looking east, circa 1925.
Photograph courtesy of Dr. G Wayne King.

The Graded School was built in 1893.

The first Florence County legislative delegation took its seat in the General Assembly of South Carolina in time to vote for the Act Incorporating the City of Florence, which, when signed by Governor Benjamin R. Tillman (1847-1918), became law December 24, 1890. The city's population that year was 3,395, and the boundaries of the town and city remained the same. The city's first mayor was Jerome P. Chase, and D. J. Justice, Dr. Furman P. Covington, William J. Brown, and W. J. Bradford were aldermen. Bradford and his successor in office, Thomas W. Jefferson, were the last blacks to serve on the city council until 1978.

The new city faced the daunting task of making itself the political nucleus of an area composed of the hinterlands of four older counties. Already there were social, economic, and political rifts dividing the yeoman farmers of the new county from the relatively more prosperous merchants and railroad men. The farmers struggled to survive, while residents of the city envisioned themselves as living in a "little Atlanta," and hoped to become as rich as the Yankees.

The depressed agricultural situation was partially the result of the sharecrop system which grew out of Reconstruction. Although wasteful of both human and natural resources, sharecropping answered the need for a new relationship between landlord and tenant in an economy where cash and credit were scarce. Cotton became the "cash crop," while corn provided sustenance for both livestock and human beings. Together, the two crops dominated farming in the Pee Dee region for nearly 75 years.

During this period, various organizations were formed to improve the lot of farmers. The Farmers' Alliance, a national organization, was introduced into South Carolina in Marion County in 1887, and by 1889, the state organizations had approximately 20,000 members. Even before the new county movement had succeeded, the Alliance had been active in Florence by backing a farmers' revolt and publishing its own newspaper.

Ben Tillman initially saw the Farmers' Alliance as a rival, but later joined forces with it, and in the 1890 election, the farmers' organizations became supporters of Tillman's bid for the South Carolina governorship. Tillman was touted by disgruntled farmers as "the only man who has the brain, the nerve, and the ability to organize the common people against the aristocracy." The citizens of Florence could scarcely pass as aristocrats, but they were perceived as the prosperous middle class, dependent on the railroads' interests.

Tillman received the Democratic nomination, but an "Independent" movement was initiated to nominate Alexander C. Haskell for governor to oppose Tillman, and a state convention was called to meet October 9, 1890, in Columbia for that purpose. Florence County held a meeting to nominate delegates to what would become known as the "Haskell Convention." General W. W. Harllee, a delegate, was elected its presiding officer.

There was little enthusiasm for Tillman in Florence, but when the Haskell ticket received the endorsement of the Republican Party, there was no hope for the latter's success. This raised the specter of a political coalition between blacks and conservative whites, which played into the hands of the growing racism being encouraged by the Tillman movement. The majority of railroad workers in Florence did not identify with the Tillman agrarian revolt, and Tillman and his candidates were consistent in attacking the railroad interests and its links with the old Bourbon politicians as oppressors of farmers.

In the event, Tillman and his ticket of statewide candidates defeated Haskell, and Tillman carried Florence County by a vote of 1,237 to 512. In the town of Florence, however, Haskell defeated Tillman by a vote of 187 to 135. The first three senators elected from Florence County, L. S. Bigham, Dr. J. O. Byrd (1856-95), and J. E. Pettigrew (1841-1909), were Tillmanites, active in the Farmers' Association. The first Tillmanite resident in Florence who succeeded in bridging the gap between county and city voters was Dr. William Ilderton (1863-1918), senator from Florence County (1898-1902). Dr. Ilderton founded one of the first hospitals in Florence, the Ilderton Infirmary, in 1907. Unfortunately, he was shot and killed by his son in the Florence County Courthouse during a domestic quarrel.

Florence police force, circa 1910. ***Photograph courtesy of Dr. G. Wayne King.***

If the farming economy was depressed in the 1890s, its prospects in the Pee Dee were improved by the introduction of a new cash crop, flue-cured tobacco. Flue-cured, or Bright, tobacco was raised successfully in Virginia and North Carolina, and it

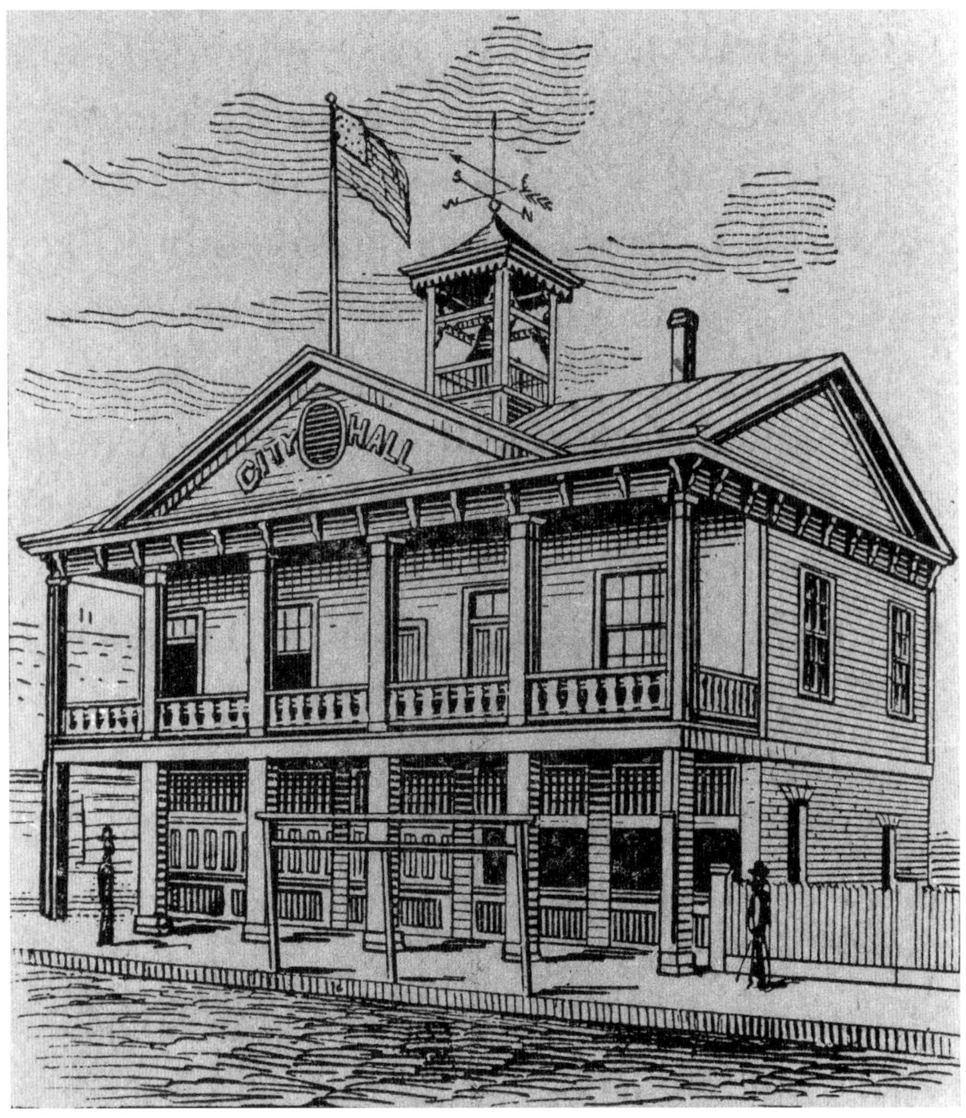

First city hall, as it appeared in 1883

was widely believed that only tobacco grown in those states had the desired flavor and aroma for cigarettes. The beginning of mass production of cigarettes caused an increased demand for Bright tobacco, but there was doubt that tobacco grown in South Carolina would have these qualities.

In 1884 Frank Mandeville Rogers Sr. (1857-1945) successfully raised an experimental crop of tobacco on his farm in the Mars Bluff area. The following year he received $600 from his three-acre crop, and it was estimated that the same acreage planted in cotton, which was averaging nine cents per pound, would have grossed only about $23 per acre. This difference in profit potential made tobacco the chief cash crop of the Pee Dee.

As more and more farmers in the upper Pee Dee turned to tobacco cultivation, the need for a local market became increasingly apparent. Rogers visited North Carolina and Virginia markets in 1890, and met with James B. Duke of the American Tobacco Company to arrange for buyers to come to South Carolina. The state's first tobacco auction warehouse opened in Florence on October 1, 1891. The Florence Tobacco Manufacturing and Warehouse Company also started a tobacco manufacturing endeavor in 1890. A small three-story tobacco factory was erected on Front Street, and its plan was to manufacture plug, twist, and smoking tobacco, but a large North Carolina manufacturer introduced a similar product at the same time, and the Florence Manufacturing Company, unable to compete, eventually closed.

The warehouses built in the 1900s gravitated toward Timmonsville, Lake City, and Pamplico. Traditionally, farmers from the county preferred taking their tobacco elsewhere because the city folks in Florence never felt comfortable with them politically or socially. Florence remained the center of the "Tobacco Belt," and in 1912, Clemson University established the Pee Dee Experiment Station near Florence to strengthen the farm economy by improving tobacco and other crops.

In December, 1887, the state legislature authorized the town of Florence to issue bonds for the purpose of securing a building site for a county courthouse and jail which, at completion, were to be presented to the new county free and clear. The lot chosen was purchased from James Allen. The lot, in the middle of the block and surrounded on two sides by stores, was on the east side of Irby Street, approximately midway between Front and Evans Streets.

The cornerstone of the courthouse was laid on August 22, 1889. While it was under construction, the commissioners rented space over Sternberger's store at the southeast corner of Front and Dargan Streets. The wooden structure burned on November 20, 1889, only a few months after the county began to conduct its activities there. Most of the county offices and records were destroyed, except for papers from the clerk's office, which were stored in Sternberger's safe. After the fire, the county offices were housed in the rear of Buchheit's store on North Dargan Street until the courthouse building was completed.

On May 31, 1890, the new courthouse was dedicated and occupied, the grounds of which would be the site of political gatherings for decades to follow. A notable encounter between the Tillman and anti-Tillman factions occurred there during a stump speaking in June, 1892. Many in the attending crowd were armed. The stump speaking was described as "the wildest and the roughest of the campaign" and a "bloody riot seemed imminent several times."

Another noteworthy encounter between the city of Florence and Governor Tillman was an incident known as the "Darlington Riot." In the fight over state controlled sale of liquor, known as the Dispensary System, there was a gun battle in the city of Darlington between local anti-Tillman citizens and representatives of the state constabulary, who were thought to be spies sent by Tillman. Several persons were killed, and Tillman declared the counties of Darlington and Florence in a state of insurrection, seizing telegraph and railroad lines to prevent the concentration of gangs bent on revenge. The situation grew more serious when many units of the state militia refused to obey Tillman's orders, so he called upon his farmer supporters, now known as "wool-hat boys," to arm themselves with shotguns and prepare to act if necessary. However, within five or six days, the Darlington Riot was over, but a generation of young

Central Hotel, located on East Evans Street. The original hotel was destroyed by a fire in 1893 which consumed 26 buildings. *Photograph courtesy of Dr. G. Wayne King.*

Florentines were admonished that if they did not behave, "A Tillman spy will get you!"

In July, 1896, at a political stump speaking at the Florence Courthouse, Governor John Gary Evans, a Tillman protege and a candidate for the United States Senate, made remarks which aroused the anger of the anti-Tillman Florentines in the audience. At one point, Evans asserted that he would carry out the policies of Ben Tillman and "force Florence to follow." This led to an exchange of blows between Evans and Judge Joseph H. Earle in which both received injuries. After

Evans left, Mayor Day had an arrest warrant served on him which Evans merely ignored because as governor he could only be tried by impeachment. This incident further divided the city from the county.

Third city hall built in 1900 on Evans Street. Watercolor by Jane Jackson.

The political schism between the city and the county, however, did nothing to harm the county's growth. In 1904 nine square miles were added from Williamsburg County, and in 1911, 92.3 square miles, including the municipality of Lake City, were joined as well. In 1921 an additional 45.3 square miles, plus the municipality of Johnsonville, increased the size of Florence County to 891.5 square miles.

The growth of the new city was not without its setbacks. Less than three years after Florence's incorporation as a city, three devastating fires swept the business district of North Dargan and Evans Streets. The first and second fires caused little damage, but while the firemen were at work on the second fire, a third building caught fire. In the third fire, 26 buildings, including the Central Hotel, city hall, Allen's Hall, and other buildings, were destroyed. The loss of the hotel, considered one of the finest in the state, was a severe blow. To make matters worse, less than two weeks later, Gamble's Hotel was destroyed by a fire.

Fires in 1896 and 1899 again leveled much of the commercial section of the city, but each time stores and hotels were rebuilt. One of the casualties of the 1899 fire was the destruction of the second city hall, which had been built on the site occupied by the first. The third city hall, which included an opera house and a town clock and bell, was designed in the Victorian neo-Gothic style which was popular at the turn of the century, and was occupied by the city council on December 3, 1900.

Despite the ravages of fire, the city was gradually acquiring creature comforts which would not be available in the surrounding countryside for the next 30 to 50 years: electric lights (1890), telephones (1894), running water and paved streets (1903), a sewerage system (1910), and gas (1912). Florence also had a movie house (1912) and a city park (1913). In 1894 the leading newspaper, the *Weekly Times,* was sold by C. H. Prince to Hartwell M. Ayer (1868-1917), who became publisher. Later the *Weekly Times* was consolidated with another newspaper and became the *Daily Times.* Another important addition to Florence was created in 1906, the first reformatory for juveniles, the South Carolina Industrial School. By coincidence, it was built on the National Cemetery Road on land donated by the Atlantic Coast Line Railroad, and included the site of the Thomas McCall plantation house which adjoined the ruins of the Confederate stockade.

The railroads' continued expansion boosted the city's economy. The Wilmington, Columbia, and Augusta Railroad merged with the Atlantic Coast Line Railroad. The North Eastern Rail Road survived as a separate entity until it merged with the Atlantic Coast Line Railroad of South Carolina in 1897, and the Cheraw and Darlington Rail Road merged in 1900. During this period, Florence was called the "Gate City," a reference to its being the point of entry into South Carolina for trains traveling from the north to the south.

Ethnic diversity was beginning to enhance the population of the city. Lebanese and Greek immigrants began settling in Florence after 1900. These migrations "followed the tracks" in the sense that they came south from New York by rail until they found a community which suited them. Many of these immigrants made outstanding contributions to the city. N. B. Baroody (1884-1987), born in Souk-el-Gharb, Lebanon, came to Florence via Richmond, opened a business in 1911, and became an outstanding merchant and civic leader. When Front Street was relocated in the 1970s, it was renamed N. B. Baroody Street in his honor. Louis Palles (1895-1969), born in Sparta, Greece, came to Florence in 1917, became a restaurateur, and was active in civic affairs for the remainder of his life. The Lebanese generally became members of the mainstream Protestant churches, but the Greeks organized a Greek Orthodox Church and, in 1962, constructed the Church of the Transfiguration.

Further affirmation of the centrality of Florence to the Pee Dee region came in 1901, when the United States Congress approved the construction of a United States District Courthouse and Post Office. To further this effort, the city bought the land on the northwest corner of Evans and Irby Streets and resold it to the federal government for one dollar. The new federal building was occupied in 1906.

Women's organizations were the first to promote civic improvement in the fast-growing city. The records from a meeting held on September 16, 1902, to establish such an agency reflect an obvious masculine "cop out," when, "after a free and enthusiastic discussion of the matter…[it was] decided to leave its operation in the hands of the women, the men promising to uphold them and assist them in every way possible." The organization accomplished

A parade of automobiles on East Evans Street. The Presbyterian Church is on the right. ***Photograph courtesy of the Florence Museum.***

Atlantic Coast Line passenger station and trains. ***Photograph courtesy of Howard Waddell.***

several important improvements, including transforming the grounds surrounding the county courthouse from an unkempt public hitching ground to a well-kept lawn with hedges and walks, establishing an Industrial Fair, adding a curb vegetable market, as well as public drinking fountains and public playgrounds. The women also revived the library, which had closed after the death of Belton O'Neall Townsend, and operated it in the new city hall building. Literary, artistic, and cultural activities also were left, by tacit consent, to feminine literary, garden, and music clubs. The Research Club, organized in 1909, was followed by the Renaissance Club in 1916. These organizations were to become important forces in the city's development.

After the State Constitution of 1895 sanctioned segregated public education, the all-white public schools began to expand. Prior to that, in 1892, a three-story brick building with eight classrooms for white children had been built on the north side of Cheves Street between Dargan Street and the railroad tracks. Black children still attended Wilson School, at its site on North Irby Street.

The Atlantic Coast Line Railroad moved its passenger station to a location several blocks east of the Church Street station in 1906. With it went the restaurant which had been operated first by Clarence Gresham and later by his son-in-law J. W. Ivey (1876-1932). The restaurant, which served only breakfast and dinner, became popular with local citizens and railroad travelers. Black waiters in white coats greeted incoming trains ringing large dinner bells, and passengers and crew disembarked to eat while the train was being serviced. The restaurant ceased operations about 1927, when dining cars became available.

In January, 1908, a second school for white children, "Central School" on Dargan Street between Palmetto and Pine Streets, now known as the Poynor School Building, was completed and dedicated. Central School was regarded as one of the finest new school buildings in the state, and had 600 white students in attendance. The first official visit to Florence by a sitting president of the United States took place at Central School. On November 8, 1909, at the invitation of the Florence Board of

Trade, President William H. Taft spoke to "an immense throng" and ate pine bark fish stew with the local citizens.

The architect for Central School was Charles Coker Wilson, an indication of the growing prosperity and sophistication of Florence. Wilson, one of the state's outstanding architects, was also the architect for the second church built by the Baptists at the corner of Palmetto and Irby Streets in 1893, and for the second church built by the Presbyterians on East Evans Street in 1904. A more modest building was the second church of Saint John's Episcopal Church on Dargan Street, built in 1889. The Lutheran Church, organized in 1896, built a church in 1908, at the corner of Palmetto Street and Railroad Avenue.

The population of the city of Florence nearly doubled in the last decade of the nineteenth century and the first decade of the twentieth century: from 4,647 in 1890, to 7,657 in 1910. Florence, as a consequence, was increasingly referred to as the "Magic City." A board of trade had been organized in the 1890s to promote commercial growth, and several industries made starts in Florence around the turn of the century, but most failed. One that did succeed was the Florence Cotton Oil Company, founded in 1902, which received patronage for many years from farmers in the area.

Another successful opening which foreshadowed the future came in October, 1909, when S. H. Kress & Company bought land on Evans Street and shortly thereafter began operating what was known as a "five-and-tencents store." It marked the advent of nationally operated chain stores on the Florence scene.

The city's growth followed the new passenger station eastward. Park School, later named Harllee School in honor of Margaret L. Harllee (1870-1947), became the elementary school for white children in 1915. Its location in East Florence was evidence of the city's continued growth in that direction.

Florence Graded School (Central School) built in 1906, now Poynor Adult Education Center. ***Photograph courtesy of Dr. G. Wayne King.***

Chapter Seven

World War I, Cultural Beginnings and Depression

(1917-41)

Interior of the Blue Bird Tea Room.
Photograph courtesy of the Florence Museum.

During World War I, the city of Florence became, again, an important railroad terminal. By December, 1917, the nation's transportation system was on the verge of collapse due to congestion. President Wilson's newly established Railroad Administration placed all railways under government control, and for 11 months they operated as a single system. The paternalism of management and the fraternalism of labor began to disappear from Florence's railroad community.

Servicemen visit with a volunteer from the Blue Bird Tea Room. ***Photograph courtesy of the Florence Museum.***

The war effort required the organization of a local draft board, and citizens were exhorted to buy victory bonds and plant "victory gardens." A Florence chapter of the American Red Cross was founded, and the League for Women's Service was mobilized for the war effort. Jane Beverly Evans was active in the League statewide, and a local chapter was organized in March, 1917. Mrs. D. M. McEachin was elected chairman.

One particular project, which involved a group of eight women, was operating a tea room to serve meals to local patrons and soldiers passing through Florence. Named the "Blue Bird Tea Room," its organization was unconventional in that each woman

Locomotive of the Atlantic Coast Line in 1930. ***Photograph courtesy of Howard Waddell.***

took a day running it, brought her own servant to do the cooking, and served whatever menu she deemed appropriate. Volunteers served the meals. The tea room was successful and continued its operations for a time after the war, serving meals to the sick during the influenza epidemic.

During World War I, 1,941 men from Florence County served in the military. In a strange analogy to the Civil War experience, Florence's harshest encounter with World War I was death by disease. Influenza made its first Florence appearance late in October, 1918, when a traveling salesman became ill and died. Thereafter, during the next six months of the epidemic of 1918-19, there were 3,487 cases reported in Florence County and 142 deaths. By comparison, and with no attempt to minimize the tragedy of any who died, 13 men in the armed services from Florence County died in combat or from wounds received in combat; 2 were killed in accidents, and 56 died of pneumonia or other diseases. Two of those who died, Fred H. Sexton and M. Wilbur Jones, are memorialized by the naming of American Legion posts in Florence and Lake City.

In 1920 the population of the city was 10,968. Increasingly, the city adopted the ways and the institutions of the national culture. The movement toward becoming a part of the national social and business scene was evidenced by the organization of men's service clubs. Jefferson Boone Aiken Sr. (1889-1978), a successful businessman, entrepreneur, and banker, was instrumental in organizing the first of these, the Rotary Club, late in 1919. The Kiwanis Club and the Lions Club followed in 1923. Service clubs channelled masculine interests and efforts into many worthwhile civic projects.

Encouraged by the passage of the Nineteenth Amendment to the Constitution of the United States, women began to play a more aggressive role in political affairs. As a sign of the growing political awareness of women in Florence, Roberta Muldrow Brown (1880-1969) ran for mayor in 1925. She was not successful. It was not until 1953 that Maye W. Stevenson (1892-1984) became the first female member of the city council.

The bitterness of labor disputes reached Florence on July 1, 1922, when 700 workers in the Atlantic Coast Line shops went on strike. The strike did not have its genesis in any specific local complaint, but was part of a national effort by the union. When it failed, more than 100 men lost their jobs. They, with their families, left Florence to seek employment. Their absence created a tear in the social fabric of Florence which would take years to mend. The replacement workers, brought in to break the strike, were often referred to by other railroad workers as "Roebucks," implying that they had been ordered through a catalogue.

Another unpleasant aspect of the post-World War I period was the decline of agriculture. In the years after the war, farm prices deflated, while farm costs continued to rise. As the 1920s progressed, the situation did not improve, so that when the Great Depression came, it merely exacerbated the already desperate economic plight of the farmer.

Significant advances were made on behalf of education, however, when Florence High School opened in 1921. At the time, the school was regarded as one of the most modern in the state. Later, the school was renamed McClenaghan High School, in honor of John C. McClenaghan, a railroad conductor and school board chairman and member for many years. Another building, initially named Eastside Elementary School, was built as an elementary school for black children on East Cheves Street. The name was changed to Holmes School to recognize the civic contributions of Dr. William F. Holmes (1868-1938), former school principal of Wilson School, and later, a practicing physician.

Dr. Holmes and his contemporary, Dr. James R. Levy (1861-1936), were leaders in the black community. Denied the opportunity to compete with white professionals and politicians, blacks found that their advancement in the academic, ministerial, and medical fields were avenues to success and recognition, even in a segregated society. Levy Park in north Florence was named for Dr. Levy, and his residence, built in 1894, was moved to the campus of McLeod Regional Medical Center in 1991, where it is used as a meeting place for various organizations.

In the 1920s, the residential development of Florence began a steady movement westward. This was demonstrated by the construction, in 1927, of another white elementary school, Circle School, later changed to McKenzie School in honor of Florence McKenzie (1871-1942), a teacher and principal of Circle School.

There were stirrings of interest in a theater which, of necessity, involved male participation. In 1923 a group calling themselves the Community Players began putting on plays on the lawn and front porch of James M. Lynch (d. 1979), the group's chief organizer. These productions were moved to the Pinewood Club, a log building

Atlantic Coast Line passenger station, circa 1925. *Photograph courtesy of Howard Waddell.*

Southern Motor Car Company's garage. ***Photograph courtesy of Dr. G. Wayne King.***

located at Five Points, a short distance from Palmetto Street, in the area of Rainbow Drive. It was used by various groups for dances, parties, and by the new theater company which then took the name "The Pinewood Players." In 1927 the Pinewood Players' theatrical productions were staged in the Y.M.C.A. building on Church Street, which had been opened in 1921. However, after 1930, the group no longer produced any plays.

The opening of the Florence Library on November 4, 1925, was a major civic and cultural advance. The library became a nucleus of cultural development and activities, including the Florence Museum and Francis Marion University. A referendum was necessary to authorize a tax levy not in excess of three mills to support the library. The successful result of the referendum was due, in large part, to the active support of women in organizing and managing it.

Under the enabling legislation, the library was placed under the control of the Florence City Schools. What began as an important organizational vehicle to promote the library, eventually, became a hindrance to its growth. The library's collection had only increased to 35,000 volumes by 1940. It continued, however, to be an important community center, containing an auditorium with a seating capacity of 300, dining room, assembly room, and kitchen.

The introduction of automobiles in the early 1900s, with the attendant garages, filling stations, and repair shops, spelled the doom of the numerous livery stables which had been a vital part of life in the city, and also contributed to the decline of the railroads. The growing use of motor transportation mandated the improvement of the roads. The first paved road was constructed between Florence and

Timmonsville in 1920, and was hailed as "Florence's Appian Way." The connection of towns was the main objective, and by 1929, there were paved roads to Timmonsville, Darlington, and Marion, and one long stretch roughly parallel to the tracks of the Atlantic Coast Line Railroad, which connected Florence to Kingstree and Charleston.

One vital improvement in the transportation system was the replacement of the ferry over the Pee Dee River at Mars Bluff by a bridge in 1923. The regional importance of the bridge is apparent in the first legislative act in 1920, which required Florence, Marion, Dillon, Berkley, and Charleston Counties to participate financially in the bridge's construction. This effort failed, and by act of the legislature in 1922, Florence and Marion Counties were authorized to construct and operate a toll bridge over the Pee Dee.

The passage of the "Pay-as-You-go" bill enacted in 1924 transferred the main burden of financing and maintaining roads from the counties to the State Highway Department. This program was augmented in 1929 by adopting a "build-now-pay-later" policy, with a gasoline tax enacted to finance road building. Gradually, paved roads were extended to rural areas.

Florentines demonstrated interest in air travel during this period as well. Prior to 1928, there were two landing strips in the western area outside of the city. The first was located in the vicinity of Five Points, and the second was between Palmetto and Evans Streets, several blocks south of Five Points. In 1928 the city acquired land east of the city limits for the purpose of maintaining a municipal airport. This became the nucleus of the present airport, named Gilbert Field in honor of Herbert K. Gilbert (1873-1958), a railroad man who served as mayor in the years 1907-13, 1917-21, and 1925-35.

The economic hardships of the Great Depression began early in Florence. On October 28, 1928, the Bank of Florence, established in 1888, suspended its business and placed its affairs in the hands of the state bank examiner. On hearing the news, men and women rushed to the bank hoping to withdraw their deposits. Their efforts were in vain, for the bank never reopened.

Florence County, already a depressed area, suffered additional economic woes. The city and the Pee Dee region, however, greatly benefitted from federal reform legislation passed to help the nation recover. Examples of this aid were the buildings built or

Two youngsters take to their bikes in a parade down Evans Street. ***Photograph courtesy of Dr. G. Wayne King.***

Parade in progress on Evans Street looking west. *Photograph courtesy of Dr. G. Wayne King.*

remodeled with Works Progress Administration (WPA) funds. An agricultural building was built on South Irby Street to house the office of the Agricultural Stabilization and Conservation Service, which provided price supports for crops, while limiting production through acreage allotment and marketing quotas. The Florence County Courthouse was extensively remodeled in 1936. A new building for McLeod Infirmary was also constructed that year.

The city park was improved with WPA funds, and a one-room white frame building in which Henry Timrod (1829-67), Poet Laureate of the Confederacy, taught school in 1859 was moved to Florence, and the park renamed Timrod Park. The WPA funded improvements to the municipal airport, purchased a bookmobile for the Florence Library, made art exhibits available to the Florence Museum, and implemented a paving program for the city and county which included extended sidewalks in the city.

In 1930 the population of Florence was 14,774, and despite the economic depression, interest in cultural activities was increasing. A series of community concerts was sponsored by voluntary contributions. Music clubs were organized, and concerts were given in the high school and in the small auditorium of the Florence Library.

The Florence Museum was incorporated in 1936. The initial collections of the museum were bought by Jane Evans from the Santa Fe Museum in 1925, using funds from the Blue Bird Tea Room. This collection was eventu-

The residence of Sanborn Chase became the Florence Museum in 1952. ***Photograph courtesy of the Florence Museum.***

ally put on display in the basement of the library in 1939. By then, the museum's collection contained a notable exhibit of southwestern Indian pottery as well as material purchased from a former missionary to China, Florence Nightingale League. The museum's display cases were purchased with donations from the Evans family and other citizens of Florence.

There was a revival of amateur theatricals, then called the Florence Little Theater Guild. Sanborn Chase (1919-61) organized this effort, and the group's first production was held at his home on Spruce Street, now the Florence Museum, in August, 1939. Productions continued at Florence High School until World War II hastened their demise.

In 1940 the population of the city was 16,054. In the decade between 1930 and 1940, the population increased by 8 percent as compared with a 26 percent growth in the previous decade. One of the projects of the WPA, the Federal Writers' Project, published in 1941 *South Carolina, A Guide to the Palmetto State.* The publication includes a brief description of Florence during the 1930s. "The business district differs from the shopping areas in hundreds of other small cities in the Southeast only by its atmosphere of busy activity, for Florence is the trade center for several surrounding counties. One six-story structure soars ambitiously above the buildings on Evans Street, the retail thoroughfare… . West Florence is the popular residence section, in which extensive lawns, flower gardens, and well kept streets shaded by oaks make an attractive setting for an unusual number of brick dwellings, though back streets have the usual number of drab little houses, generally unpainted and overcrowded, for the lower classes of both races. In East Florence are the small homes owned by the hundreds of railroad shop workers, who compose a good proportion of the inhabitants."

The Guide also notes that "In addition to its railroad and agricultural interests, Florence has numerous industrial plants: one of the largest furniture factories in the State, one of the most extensive bakeries in the Carolinas, the only plow factory in South Carolina, the Palmetto Nurseries, one of the largest florists' concerns in the state, and others. The annual pay roll of all industries exceeds $790,000, of which $500,000 comes from the railroad shops." The publication states that there were six bus companies serving Florence, three hotels and several tourists' homes, a board of trade with offices in City Hall, radio station WOLS (1200kc), two movie theaters, a municipal pool, tennis courts and a softball field in the city park, Florence Country Club (incorporated in 1924), and an annual Pee Dee Fair. The Farm Women's Community Market, located next to the Courthouse, is described as a brick building with 65 stalls where farm women, under the direction of the Home Demonstration Agent, sell farm products, homemade edibles, and handiwork.

There was a foreshadowing of World War II during 1940-41, when the city sought the establishment of a military base. The culmination of this effort came in November, 1941, when the Army's 30th Pursuit Squadron and the 31st Pursuit Group were based at the Florence Airport during maneuvers. The Japanese attack on Pearl Harbor was only weeks away.

Zeigler's Drug Store at the corner of Dargan and Evans Streets. Dr. Roland Zeigler *(left)* served as mayor of Florence from 1943 to 1947. *Photograph courtesy of Dr. G. Wayne King.*

Extra! Morning
JAPS
WAR ON

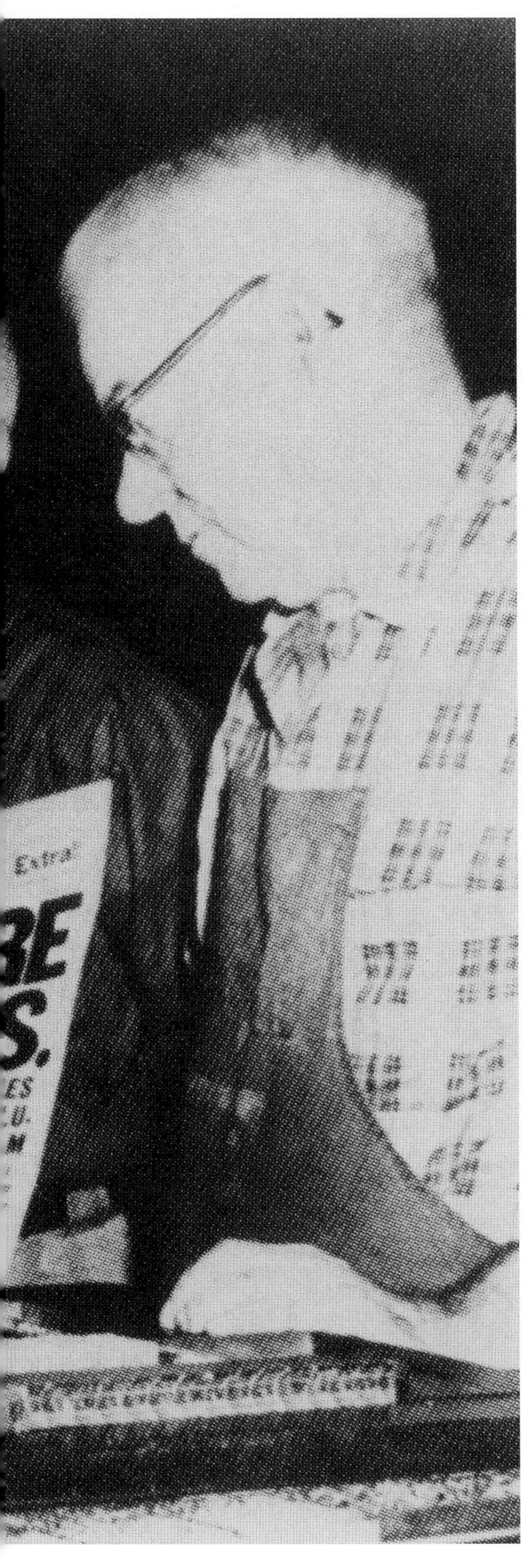

Chapter Eight

World War II and Expansion of Industrial Base

(1942-present)

Employees of the *Florence Morning News* inspect the EXTRA edition announcing the commencement of World War II.
Photograph courtesy of Dr. G. Wayne King.

Within a month of the United States' entrance into World War II, the city purchased 200 acres at the airfield for a camp to house 2,700 members of the Army Air Force. In February, 1942, an Army Air Force Pursuit Group moved in, and left in April, leaving only a Signal Group and other smaller units. By October, the city had acquired additional land to expand the old landing field, and the title was transferred to the federal government. Congress appropriated over two million dollars to improve runways and construct warehouses, medical facilities, barracks, officers' quarters, and repair shops to accommodate approximately 5,000 men.

The installation was named Florence Army Air Base, and its chief mission was to conduct a training program for troop carriers. Units using P-39 fighters were the first trained, followed by the Air Transport Command, which flew DC-3s, and a unit of gliders. These were followed by A-20 bombers, part of the 411th Bomber Group. At the end of the war, B-25 bomber pilots were being trained in Florence. In an odd historical parallel, during the last year of the war, 30 to 40 German prisoners were imprisoned at the Florence Army Air Base within a mile of the Civil War stockade.

By September, 1945, the air base was put on inactive status. The Army attempted to acquire it for a perma-

Dance held for servicemen in Florence during World War II. ***Photograph courtesy of Dr. G. Wayne King.***

nent base, but the effort failed. In April, 1946, most of the land was returned to the city with a provision that the government could reclaim it in a national emergency. There were slightly more than 400 acres in the original municipal airfield, and the Army had added approximately 1,200 acres, creating an airport complex encompassing more than 1,600 acres. Among the nonaviation uses of the airport property that began in 1946 were industrial companies, commercial strip development, warehouses, and an Air Missile Museum.

The social impact of the air base on Florence was tremendous. For four years, the local population was exposed to young people of varied backgrounds from all over the country. The experience became a major force in bringing the Florence community into the mainstream of twentieth-century American life, a key objective of Florence's postwar leaders. World War II brought about a unified effort in Florence and the South and renewed the region's sense of patriotism and American identity that had been uncertain since the Civil War.

The number of Florence men killed in the armed services was greater than in World War I. It is estimated that 31 Florence residents died on active duty. The stadium erected on property which had been part of the Florence Army Air Base was built as a memorial to all Florentines who served in World War II. In addition, the National Cemetery, once the burial ground for Union soldiers, was increasingly used by area residents as the burial ground for veterans of all wars.

In 1950 the city's population had increased to 22,513. A series of annexations expanded the city westward after the war. The circular city limits, established in 1871, enclosed 2,010 acres. Beginning in 1948, the city limits increased, and now encompasses 9,978 acres.

Theodore Lester (1908-89) served in the U.S. Army during World War II. Lester returned to Florence, became a prominent educator and the first black man elected to the school board of Florence School District Number One. *Photograph courtesy of Dr. G. Wayne King.*

Most noteworthy, however, was the development of a new industrial base after the war. Florence Manufacturing Company and Wentworth Manufacturing Company, both sewing operations for the garment industry, were part of this movement. The purchase of land by DuPont, in 1950, signaled even broader industrial expansion. Soon thereafter, Koppers Company,

Blacks became police officers. ***Photograph courtesy of Dr. G. Wayne King.***

Inc., chartered in 1954, built a wood preserving plant to process poles, piling, cross ties, and fence posts. Inexorably, the railroads were losing their position to new industry.

There was also an outburst of cultural activity in the post-war years. During the period from 1941 to 1946, the Little Theater remained dormant, but in December, 1947, a play was produced in the old air base theater, which the city made available to the Florence Little Theater Guild. Three or four plays were produced each year, and several plays were written by a member of the group. The air base theater served as its home until 1968, when a modern theater was constructed on the Old Timmonsville Highway with a seating capacity of approximately 400.

The Florence Civic Orchestra, initially a municipal band, was organized in 1948, with Haldane Strain (1916-1976) as conductor. The group of 37 musicians presented its first concert in Lake City in 1949. The orchestra now performs a series of yearly concerts. In addition, the Florence Choral Society of the 1950s was the predecessor of the Masterworks Choir, organized in 1980. Members of the Masterworks Choir come from Florence and the Pee Dee region. Under the direction of William Mills, the choir produces public concerts each year.

Young adults in Florence became increasingly involved in civic organizations. The Junior Welfare League, organized in 1948, became involved in volunteer services such as the Pee Dee Coalition, Manna House, and Rescue Mission. In 1989 the League was accepted by the Association of Junior Leagues International and became The Junior League of Florence, Inc. The Florence Junior Chamber of Commerce, for men, initially organized in 1939, became reactivated, and stressed self-improvement, community awareness, and fellowship.

A significant program to help young boys was created by the incorporation of the Pee Dee Area Big Brothers Association in July, 1953. The organization, initially affiliated with the national organization, was the first in the South and the first located in a predominantly rural area. It now has over 300 Little Brothers and is affiliated with a Big Sisters organization.

The growing need for helping organizations led to the formation of the United Fund for Greater Florence. Dr. Walter R. Mead (1897-1976), former treasurer of the Community Chest organization, spearheaded this effort, and in 1954 led a successful campaign to aid 12 agencies. By 1956 there were 21 agencies served, and a payroll deduction plan was established. The name changed to the United Way of Florence County in 1978, with approximately 30 agencies served. The Boy Scouts, organized in 1928, and the Girl Scouts, organized in 1933, are two of the many organizations supported by the United Way.

In 1952 the Florence Museum purchased, with a donation from Thomas Evans, brother of Jane B. Evans, the Sanborn Chase Residence at Graham and Spruce Streets. The renovated building opened in October, 1953. The museum's collections have expanded to include exhibits of local and regional interest, and its opening at the present location led to a new appreciation for visual arts in Florence. Accomplished artists in the Pee Dee began exhibiting in the museum, which has since acquired a collection of modern South Carolina artists. This collection includes paintings by William Johnson (1901-1970), a native of Florence and one of the most important black American painters.

With the increase in the number of cultural organizations, an Arts Council was established in 1984 to promote and facilitate the practice, performance, and appreciation of the arts in the Florence area. There are 50 member organizations of the Arts Council, including the Florence Ballet Company, the Florence Artists Guild, and the eBushua Foundation, organized to promote the preservation of Afro-American heritage through special performances and presentations.

The school integration decision of 1954 created a crisis in Florence and the South similar to that experienced during Reconstruction. The *Florence Morning News* was in the forefront of the angry debate which threatened to disrupt the orderly progress of the city. Its young editor, John H. "Jack" O'Dowd (1926-86), angered conservative white citizens by his editorials urging the acceptance of integration as the law of the land. For his enlightened opinions, he was vilified by the vast majority of the white community. Although he was the son of the publisher and owner of the newspaper, he aroused so much antagonism by his editorials that in 1956 his father asked him to resign, and he moved out of the state.

Nevertheless, other voices of moderation were beginning to be heard. In 1957 a group of Christian ministers, including a native Florentine, the Reverend Larry A. Jackson, and the Rector of Saint John's Episcopal Church, the Reverend Joseph R. Horn III (1921-71), published a controversial pamphlet entitled *South Carolinians Speak* and subtitled "A Moderate Approach to Race Relations." It consisted of 12 articles written by South Carolinians urging a reasoned approach to the integration controversy. One of the contributors was John W. Moore (1878-1965), former superintendent of the Florence City Schools, for whom Moore Intermediate School is named.

James A. Rogers (1905-90), who returned as editor of the *Florence Morning News* in 1957, organized a retreat at Litchfield Beach, South Carolina, in 1963. The gathering included many of the white businessmen, civic leaders, and politicians in Florence. What developed as a result of the retreat was known as "The Spirit of Litchfield." The majority of those attending resolved to foster a positive attitude toward public school integration and the removal of segregation laws from the city's ordinances. Beginning in 1959, the Aiken Foundation, established by J. Boone Aiken Sr. in 1947, donated grants for a series of community seminars which encouraged a rational approach to integration.

The library went through a transformation as an indirect result of the integration crisis. In 1961 the state legislature transferred control from the

Old and new locomotives. ***Photograph courtesy of Howard Waddell.***

Florence District One School Board to an independent Library Board. In 1964 the Florence Public Library and the Florence County Circulating Library merged to provide a unified public library system in Florence County. Lake City and Johnsonville, which had established libraries, joined the county library that year, and branches were established in Pamplico in 1968 and Timmonsville in 1971. The county library has been designated by the South Carolina Library as one of three Area Reference Resource Centers in South Carolina with a collection of over 150,000 volumes.

A hundred years after the end of the Civil War, the composition of political parties began to change. From 1895 to 1966, nomination by the Democratic Party was deemed tantamount to election. However, beginning in 1966, the South Carolina Republican Party began to field candidates which transferred the crux of the election process from the primary to the general election. Blacks in overwhelming numbers began to vote for the Democratic Party's candidates, while the Republican Party increasingly attracted white voters. The election of blacks to public office and their acceptance in the workforce on an equal basis gradually become commonplace. In 1977 the first blacks in this century elected to city council were Mordecai C. Johnson (1931-94), an attorney, and the Reverend John A. Sellers. Since then, there have been two black members of city council. In 1991 John R. Outlaw was the first white Republican to be elected to city council.

Florence is designated an All-America City. *Left to right*: Powell Black, city manager, Fred Samara, president of the Chamber of Commerce, and Mayor David McLeod.

The decades after World War II brought about an increase in tourism. Florence, located midway between New York and Miami, was the logical stopping place for automobile traffic using U.S. 301, a major north-south highway. The building of motels, the widening of city streets, and construction of a major underpass on Palmetto Street were evidence of the effort to accommodate the traveling public.

In 1960 the population of Florence was 24,722. It was on the threshold of receiving the accolade of being an exemplary American city. In 1965 Florence was designated an All-America City, an award given annually to 10 cities by *Look* magazine.

The award's announcement was the culmination of efforts begun 100 years before to put the town of Florence in the mainstream of American municipal life. The recognition served to boost efforts to attract industry to the Florence area. While many organizations and individuals contributed to making the award a reality, it represented the crowning achievement of Mayor David H. McLeod (1915-86) during his administration as mayor.

The city council members were Maitland S. Chase Jr. (1909-70), Dennis D. O'Brien (1916-73), R. Weston Patterson, and J. Madison Rainwater.

Florence's leaders recognized that if the city was to provide a labor source for the rapid industrialization taking place, educational opportunities would have to be expanded. In 1957 Francis Marion University began as a two-year college branch of the University of South Carolina, its classrooms in the basement of the library vacated by the Florence Museum. The Florence Darlington Technical Educational Center opened in September, 1964.

Events were taking place on the state and national level which changed the relationship between the city and county. In 1964 the United States Supreme Court's "one man, one vote" interpretation of the Fourteenth Amendment eliminated the county as a significant election district for the state legislature. Increasingly, local, state, and congressional districts and precincts were tailored to ensure ethnic representation without regard for county boundaries.

The passage of the "Home Rule Act" in 1975 allowed counties to act as municipal corporations with power to pass ordinances for the government of the county for the first time in the state's history. Counties and cities began to recognize the savings which would be gained by eliminating duplication services. This led to a movement toward consolidation. The movement had been anticipated in Florence, where the Florence City-County Building Commission, created by an act of the legislature in 1968, was empowered to erect a building housing the offices of both bodies. Construction of the Florence City-County Complex commenced in 1970, and the county courthouse and city hall were razed to provide parking spaces for the new building. The Complex was opened in 1971. Since that time, a separate detention center for the city and county has been built at Effingham, and a separate building to house the Magistrate's Court has been built on Dargan Street on the site of the store in which the first records of the county were housed.

A modern Amtrak passenger train. ***Photograph courtesy of Howard Waddell.***

The United States District Courthouse was moved to the McMillan Building, named for Congressman John L. McMillan (1898-1979), in 1977. Although a branch of the United States Post Office was maintained in the McMillan Building, the main post office was relocated westward to the corner of Cashua Drive and West Evans Streets.

In 1969 an act of the legislature created a city and county Airport Commission to operate the Florence airport. It was a joint project, and the city transferred half ownership in the airport property to Florence County. In 1990 a further attempt was made to involve the Pee Dee region in the airport's operation. The legislature created the Pee Dee Regional Airport District with a nine-member commission to run the airport. The commission includes membership not only from the city and county of Florence, but also from Darlington, Marion, and Dillon Counties.

The westward and southwestern movement of Florence brought two shopping malls, the Florence Mall (1965) at Five Points, and Magnolia Mall (1979) located at the intersection of Interstates 95 and 20. The interstate highways had a tremendous impact on the development of Florence, almost as great as the building of the railroads in the 1850s. Florence is now not only the midway point on I-95, which connects Maine with Miami, but it is also the eastern terminus of I-20, which goes, by way of Atlanta, to El Paso, Texas.

There was sporadic agitation for the creation of a civic center in Florence, which came to a successful conclusion in 1990, when a 10,000-seat civic center was built on land donated by the R. P. Byrd estate. The civic center, located at the intersection of Interstates 95 and 20, is operated by a special commission responsible to both the city and the county. It is positioned to attract an audience from the entire Pee Dee region, and its existence symbolizes Florence's development as the cultural center of the Pee Dee.

Freedom Florence, a recreation facility owned by the city and consisting of a softball complex with walking trails and picnic areas on the Pamplico Highway, was opened in June, 1990. With four multipurpose playing fields, each seating 500 spectators, it has become a major attraction for the entire area.

Gardens and gardening, which had engaged the interest of many area citizens, became popular on a wider scale after World War II. Charles H. Womack (1908-88) was one of a growing number of nurserymen promoting extensive planting of azaleas and

Florence Symphony Orchestra in concert

camellias. The increased horticultural activity resulted in the spectacular beautification of Florence, and the Rotary Club, to showcase the spring floral display, instituted an annual "Beauty Trail" through the city. Nothing is more appropriate than for Florence to become what its name implies, a "city of flowers."

In 1980 Florence's population had increased to 29,894. There was a leveling off, however, in the following 10 years. The population in 1990 was 29,913. The lack of growth is partially explained by the fact that there were fewer annexations in that period, and many of the new suburban developments were located outside the city's limits. There was an incidental loss of about 50 city dwellings in the heart of East Florence when the Housing Authority of Florence razed them during a program of urban renewal. Approximately 27 acres acquired by the Housing Authority was conveyed to the city and reconveyed to the Pee Dee Regional Health Services District. A substantial portion of the cleared area was then leased to McLeod Regional Medical Center, which occupies the center of old East Florence.

The gradual decline of the railroads reached its bottom when the railroad shops in Florence were closed in May, 1990. All shop buildings were dismantled, and tracks were removed in February, 1992. The original main line of the Wilmington and Manchester survived only as the portion of the railroad between Florence and the town of Pee Dee in Marion County. After a series of mergers, the freight service of the railroad became a part of CSX Transportation, Inc. Its Florence office is the headquarters for the "Florence Service Lane," and CSX has approximately 300 employees in the Service Lane between Savannah, Georgia, and Richmond, Virginia. The federally controlled "intercity rail passenger service," Amtrak, leases office space in the old passenger station of the Atlantic Coast Line, now owned by McLeod Regional Medical Center.

First commencement after Francis Marion University became a four-year college. ***Left to right:*** **James Dickey, President W.D. Smith, Tony Watkins, and James Rogers.** ***Photograph courtesy of Dr. G. Wayne King.***

The history of Florence, which began with three railroads, does not end with their decline. A galaxy of industries and services, homegrown and exotic, gradually replaced railroads as the economic base of Florence's growth. For nearly 150 years Florence sought to become a vibrant American city. Open to new ideas, adapting to change, always welcoming newcomers, yearning for the humane characteristics of cosmopolitan life, religious in form and substance, and lucky in her geographical location—Florence carries into the next century a renaissance spirit, an optimistic vision of a dynamic, beautiful city, offering hope for regeneration and growth to the Pee Dee region.

Florence County is comprised of five school districts serving nearly 25,000 students. The education of the county's young people remains a high priority. *Photograph courtesy of Carolina Power & Light.*

Florence City-County Civic Center. *Photograph courtesy of Carolina Power & Light.*

The Columns features Greek Revival architecture, a style popular among plantation homes in the 1850s. ***Photograph courtesy of Carolina Power & Light.***

Individuals and families will find recreational variety in the 15 parks located throughout Florence County. Timrod Park is pictured here. ***Photograph courtesy of Carolina Power & Light.***

The primary influence of the railroads on early Florence County is recalled by this mural located in downtown Florence. ***Photograph courtesy of Carolina Power & Light.***

Florence County offers cultural opportunities for all ages.
Photograph courtesy of Carolina Power & Light.

A strategic location at I-95 and I-20 has established Florence County as the business center of the Pee Dee region. *Photograph courtesy of Carolina Power & Light.*

The premier recreational complex, Freedom Florence, offers multipurpose fields, walking trails, and picnic areas. *Photograph courtesy of Carolina Power & Light.*

Downtown Florence, a city with a renaissance spirit all its own. ***Photograph courtesy of Carolina Power & Light.***

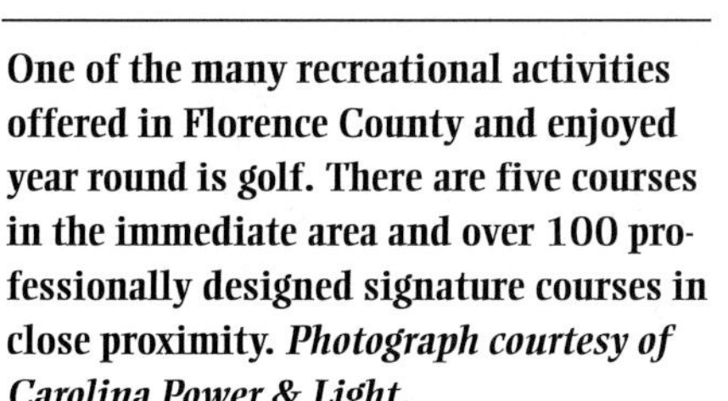

One of the many recreational activities offered in Florence County and enjoyed year round is golf. There are five courses in the immediate area and over 100 professionally designed signature courses in close proximity. ***Photograph courtesy of Carolina Power & Light.***

Fish, canoe, or stroll the nature trails of the area's two state parks. ***Photograph courtesy of Carolina Power & Light.***

A Civil War reenactment is held biannually at the Columns. ***Photograph courtesy of Carolina Power & Light.***

Florence Regional Airport, pictured at dusk, has recently undertaken multimillion-dollar renovations.

KRESS'
5-10-25 CENT STORE

Chapter Nine

Partners in Progress

Photographs on pages 120 and 138 by Kris Trahnstrom

Photograph on page 158 courtesy of Darlington Raceway

The S. H. Kress Store on West Evans Street in downtown Florence

Mount Hope Cemetery

On August 17, 1880, a group of citizens met in the office of Jerome P. Chase to consider developing a cemetery to meet the needs of the rapidly growing town. The two existing cemeteries, considered inadequate, were the Presbyterian churchyard cemetery and the Fraternal Burying Ground.

The group formed a corporation named Mount Hope Cemetery Association, which was chartered on March 2, 1881, and stock was sold to local citizens. On October 18, 1881, Mount Hope bought 203 acres owned by Mary A. E. Harrell, inherited from her father, James A. Pettigrew, located on the south side of Mars Bluff Road, later Cherokee Road. The tract was bordered on the north by Cherokee Road, on the south by Jefferies Creek, on the east to the Northeastern Rail Road, and on the west by Gully Branch.

With considerably more land than was needed for the cemetery, the cemetery was developed in the northeastern corner with a main entrance at the end of South Dargan Street, and lots were laid out eastward to the railroad. The undeveloped acreage was leased out for agricultural use.

Some of the initial burials involved moving graves from the First Presbyterian churchyard, after the church relocated on East Evans Street. Lack of space and interest caused the eventual abandonment of the Fraternal Burying Ground, and many of its graves were moved to Mount Hope. The remains of the 64 Confederate soldiers who died in Florence during the Civil War were moved and reinterred in a common grave at Mount Hope, and the monument placed in the Presbyterian churchyard in 1882 was moved and placed over their graves. There are 128 other Confederate veterans buried in the cemetery. In 1949 the Woodland Garden Club placed a monument in Mount Hope in memory of the 30 Florence men who died in service during World War II.

At the time the property was acquired, Irby Street terminated at Cherokee Road. The road to Lake City was an extension of Church Street to Coles Crossroads. In 1912 the state highway department extended Irby Street south through Mount Hope's property, connecting Irby Street with Coles Crossroads. This divided the cemetery's property. The Irby Street property continued to be leased for agricultural use until 1963, when a ground lease was given for property on the west side of the street to Horne's Motel. This was followed with ground leases for various other commercial properties along both sides of Irby Street.

The portion of the property used for grave sites contains 90 acres, enough land to supply the community's needs for burial spaces for well into the twenty-first century. Funds from lot sales have been used to improve the cemetery and to establish a perpetual care fund, one of the largest funds in South Carolina. Recent improvements and additions have been a chapel mausoleum added in 1989, landscape improvements with a paved main entry road lined with live oaks, a new entrance gate, and, in 1994, a new brick wall along Cherokee Road. Through 1995, there have been approximately 12,000 burials in the cemetery.

The founders of Mount Hope stated that their purpose was to create a necropolis of "first-class elegance." That is still its objective.

City of Florence

A dynamic community of unique and diverse business opportunity, the city of Florence is a modern-day success story of business achievement and community success. From its beginning as a railroad junction with large repair shops, the city has encouraged a favorable business climate. Support of business has been, and continues to be, a primary objective of the mayor and city council.

Two main issues which face Florence and other local municipal governments in South Carolina are city-county efforts to consolidate services and the improvement of city-county relations. The consolidation of city-county services reached a high point when the Florence City-County Complex was

The Florence City-County Complex

opened in 1972. Here was tangible proof that by pooling efforts the two governmental agencies could achieve savings of money and effort.

The years ahead promise a new chapter in improved relations between the city and county. Since 1921, the city has been operated under the council-manager form of government. Florence has been fortunate in the quality of men who have served as city managers. One of these, Thomas W. Edwards Jr., a native of the Pee Dee region, was appointed city manager in September, 1977, and resigned in December, 1995, to accept the position of administrator for Florence County. Edwards held the position of city mana-ger longer than any of his predecessors, and he is the only former city manager who has become administrator for Florence County. His appointment as county administrator promises a new era both in consolidation of city-county services and in harmonious city-county relations generally.

Freedom Florence Recreational Complex

There has been a great deal of discussion about keeping governmental expenditures within the CPI and not raising taxes in an amount greater than the CPI. For the period of fiscal year 1993-94, the city of Florence has not only kept expenditures within the CPI, but it has also operated between the CPI.

In 1979 the city of Florence received, in actual dollars, approximately $2.7 million from property tax revenues. In fiscal year 1995-96, and after the Local Option Sales Tax (L.O.S.T.) credit, the anticipated property tax revenues derived from city taxpayers is estimated to be approximately $2.4 million.

The budget for fiscal year 1995-96 proposed that the current tax rate be reduced to 73.4 mills, better to reflect revenue needs. In addition, the proposed budget for fiscal year 1996-97 anticipates a further reduction of a projected 5 mills. In addition to the property tax decrease, an elimination of the recycling fee was accomplished. The proposed tax reductions and the tax credits derived from the Local Option Sales Tax place the taxpayers in the city of Florence in a position which has been sought after by many municipalities, but realized by few.

Through a well-organized cost reduction program in recent years, by structuring very conservative budgets, and maintaining appropriations, the city of Florence has reached a very strong and enviable position which permits, for the first time that modern records reveal, a property tax decrease.

The city of Florence was incorporated after the county of Florence was created, but the city of Florence contributed not only the leadership of the new county movement, but it also appropriated money to finance its promotion. Together, the two governments have demonstrated the ability to plan together for a better future for themselves and for the Pee Dee region.

Carolina Power & Light

In 1996 Carolina Power & Light celebrated 70 years of partnership with the people of South Carolina. While dependable electrical service is still the company's basic product, CP&L's energy goes far beyond electricity. As a company, CP&L supports economic development, education, community improvement, and the environment. As individuals, CP&L employees work hard to improve South Carolina's quality of life.

Carolina Power & Light's roots grow deep in South Carolina. In Florence, they can be traced back to 1890, when Florence Improvement and Manufacturing Company was chartered to furnish the city with lighting. The company built a small power plant and installed electric arc street lights. Company ownership was turned over to Jerome P. Chase in 1892, who sold it to Florence Power & Light Company in 1904.

Left to right: **CP&L employees Adrian Wilson, district manager, and Larry Waring, power engineer, discuss energy needs with Jim Feighery, manager of manufacturing at Amana-Raytheon Appliances in Florence.**

Florence Power & Light Company provided Florence County's first electric service in 1904. The next 22 years brought a series of purchases and mergers involving utilities in Florence, Darlington, Marion, and surrounding communities, producing electric utilities of various sizes and names. Eventually, the Florence area was served by the Yadkin River Power Company. In 1926 Yadkin River and three other utilities in the Carolinas joined to become Carolina Power & Light Company.

Today, CP&L employs more than 900 people and serves more than 152,000 customers in northeastern South Carolina. The South Carolina service area is managed through the Southern Region headquarters in Florence.

Over the years, CP&L has invested more than $1.1 billion in South Carolina capital projects, including the H. B. Robinson Nuclear Plant near Hartsville. Named for South Carolina native Henry Burton Robinson, the plant was the Southeast's first commercial nuclear reactor. At the time of its dedication in 1971, it was the largest pressurized-water reactor in the world. Nearby is the Robinson Steam Plant, a coal-fired plant that began service in 1960.

The Robinson/Darlington County Combustion Turbine Plant uses oil-and gas-fired combustion turbines to power its 11 generators. To provide for future growth, CP&L broke ground on two additional generating units at the plant in 1995, increasing the company's capital investment in South Carolina by another $65 million. The plant began commercial operation in 1973.

Believing in the power of growing, vibrant communities, CP&L works closely with state and local economic development organizations to recruit more jobs to the area and assist in the retention and expansion of existing industry. From General Electric in the 1970s, to Amana-Raytheon Appliances in the 1980s, and Roche Carolina, Inc. in the 1990s, CP&L has a long tradition of improving our community's prosperity.

CP&L provides promotional assistance to the Florence County Economic Development Authority. Resources such as brochures, videos, aerial photographs, and trade show support are valuable tools in the Authority's efforts to promote Florence County as a prime business location offering a high quality of life.

CP&L also provides engineering consultation to businesses interested in decreasing energy costs through energy-efficient lighting, equipment modifications, and other improvements. This consultation helped Tupperware Manufacturing not only keep its local plant open, but also consolidate all its operations in South Carolina.

CP&L devotes resources to the community in other ways. Its innovative "Adopt State Parks" program, the first of its kind in the country, involves hundreds of employees in improvement projects in seven state parks in the Pee Dee. CP&L employees have built picnic tables, installed bluebird houses, renovated shelters, cleared hiking paths–all to enhance the recreational and educational value of state parks.

CP&L has supported construction of 14 Habitat for Humanity homes in Florence and many others throughout the Pee Dee. Those homes meeting

CP&L linemen help keep the power flowing over the company's 8,500 miles of distribution lines in South Carolina. CP&L service continuity is a source of pride for the company and comfort for customers. Even after a massive storm like Hurricane Hugo in 1989—when nearly all of CP&L's customers were affected—CP&L workers were able to restore power to most customers in a matter of days. As a result of Hugo, CP&L workers replaced 384 transmission poles, 280 miles of conductor, and 2,300 transformers and made repairs to 48 substations, at a total cost of $11.3 million.

CP&L's "Common Sense" energy-efficiency standards will provide owners energy savings for years to come. CP&L provided consultation on the state's first "Earth Smart" Habitat home, featuring various energy-efficient systems and construction techniques for even greater energy savings.

Since 1982, CP&L's "Project Share" has provided $860,000 in heating assistance to needy families in South Carolina. Donations from CP&L employees, customers, and shareholders and various civic, church, and community groups are matched dollar-for-dollar by CP&L up to $250,000 yearly. Program costs are absorbed by CP&L and agencies allocating funds to families needing assistance during the coldest months.

Nothing is more important to a community's future than its children. To provide children with the best educational experiences, CP&L sponsors programs such as "Silence the Violence," Cities in Schools, and Junior Achievement. Many CP&L employees offer one-on-one mentoring for at-risk youth. CP&L has been instrumental in the success of the Pee Dee Education Foundation, which offers career expos, performing arts showcases, a camp for at-risk children, special financial aid software, and $125,000 in mini-grants for innovative classroom projects.

"CP&L's commitment to the foundation is indicative of its commitment to the community," said Martha Davis, executive director of the foundation. "The company is a wonderful asset to our program. It's great having access to CP&L's expertise."

Recognizing the difficulty of learning in an uncomfortably hot or cold classroom, CP&L developed the "Cool Schools 2000" program. Through energy consultations, facility evaluations, and audits, CP&L has helped Pee Dee schools renovate more than 3,000 classrooms at about one-eighth the cost of new construction. These schools have not only achieved a more favorable learning environment, but have also saved energy and tax dollars.

Committed to environmental education, CP&L contributed volunteer labor and $40,000 to Woods Bay State Park Nature Center in Florence County. The facility hosts environmental education programs for thousands of school children each year. CP&L also developed a local nature trail for physically and visually challenged children.

Perhaps the most active way in which CP&L contributes leadership to the community is through the Greater Florence Chamber of Commerce. For many years CP&L employees have devoted their time and energy to serving as officers, directors, and volunteers. This commitment on behalf of the company and its employees has helped make the city of Florence a better place to live.

Through these efforts, as well as significant participation in United Way and other programs, CP&L strives to do more than provide dependable electric service. As a South Carolina company, CP&L is committed to making our communities better and stronger for all South Carolinians.

CP&L employee Dena Altman, student Adam Drake, and teacher Charles Branch explore a nature trail for physically and visually challenged children at the Theodore Lester School in Florence. CP&L employees helped create the trail by volunteering their time and donating poles and trees.

Greater Florence Chamber of Commerce

The Greater Florence Chamber of Commerce began as a board of trade in the 1890s and became a member of the Chamber of Commerce of the United States in 1916. The chief activity of that organization was the dissemination of information about Florence. On March 23, 1925, the Chamber sponsored a visit to Florence by then Secretary of Commerce Herbert Hoover. He was entertained in the home of Dr. Frank H. McLeod and spoke at the annual banquet of the Chamber, which was held in the Atlantic Coast Line restaurant. On June 17, 1936, in the depths of the Depression, the Florence Board of Trade was incorporated. The organizers of the new corporation were Willis Gregory Sr. (1898-1956), Sam J. Royall (1889-1949), and Raymond C. Holt. Gregory, a successful merchant and distributor of seafood, became the first president. Royall was a prominent lawyer and member of the school board for whom Royal Elementary School was named. Holt was the manager of J. C. Penney Company. On the board of directors, with Royall and Holt, were D. H. McEachern, T. D. Ector, N. B. Baroody, W. A. Lewis, Oscar Furchgott, Jeter Rollins, L. C. Hite, Haskell Thomas, and Edwin Brooks. Thomas was later mayor of Florence from 1947 to 1951. Gregory served as president until 1929, when he was succeeded by John M. O'Dowd (1887-1970), publisher of the *Florence Morning News*.

On February 19, 1940, the name of the organization was changed to the Florence Chamber of Commerce. Its stated goals were "to promote the industrial, commercial, civic, and educational development of the city of Florence." D. H. McEachern (1895-1974) became the first president of the Chamber, and the decision was made to employ a director, T. J. Mitchell, who remained in that position until 1956.

The Pee Dee area showed much progress in education in the 1960s. The Florence Regional Campus of USC was opened in 1961. It later became Francis Marion University. A regional technical education center, Florence-Darlington Technical College was also formed. Both institutions were on the Chamber's agenda. *Below*, the current-day campus of Florence-Darlington Technical College and *(above right)*, Francis Marion University.

A unique feature of its operation in the 1940s, and a sign of the times, was a credit bureau. Most of the Chamber's effort in the first half of that decade was directed toward wartime priorities such as housing and community-service relations. In the second half, it assisted in getting the Army Air Base transferred to the city and attracting industry to the Florence area. Through joint efforts with the city of Florence, it was successful in getting Eastern Airlines to start operations at Gilbert Field.

In an effort to build up the industrial base of the community, local businessmen, with the Chamber's encouragement and assistance, bought property and built a plant. The building was leased to Florence Manufacturing Company, a garment sewing operation, which commenced operations in August 1947. Florence Manufacturing was a harbinger of industries to come. Dupont purchased land near Florence in 1950, and although it did not build on the site until nine years later, it became the linchpin of industrial development in the area.

The Chamber reorganized in 1956, divested itself of the credit bureau, and commenced devoting itself strictly to Chamber-related operations. Marion D. Lucas Jr. was president of the Chamber during this period, which saw a tremendous growth in the number of industries locating in the Florence area and in upgrading and expanding established industries. In 1960 Irving Blanchard replaced Mitchell as executive vice president.

The promotion and development of both Florence-Darlington Technical College and Francis Marion University were part of the Chamber's agenda. The Chamber played an important part in many projects which led to the selection of Florence as an All-America City in 1956. Among these were the efforts to get Piedmont Airlines to Florence and assisting in securing rights-of-way leading to the widening of U. S. Highway 301 from Florence to Ebenezer. The Florence Air and Missile Museum was also founded by the Chamber.

The Florence Youth Council was founded by the Chamber's Recreation Committee. The Council, made up of representatives from all the high schools for the purpose of discussing and solving problems of the teenager, has since been transferred to the city's recreation department.

The Chamber played an important role in obtaining leases on the Promenade parking area and working with the Downtown Florence Association, which is now an independent group formed for the development of the downtown area. The Cultural Committee researched and developed the Florence Arts Festival.

The Industrial Relations Division of the Chamber was formed in 1970 with the hiring of a full-time manager. This division's purpose was to work with and assist existing industry in the field of industrial and employee relations, conduct seminars for management and supervisory training, and to conduct research and surveys for industrial use. The division was financed by industries in the area and throughout Florence, Williamsburg, Marion, and Darlington Counties. It is now an independent group called the Employers Association. Today, the Chamber and the Employers Association work closely together and cosponsor seminars and roundtable discussions.

In 1985, under the leadership of Rod Jernigan and Carlos Hanna, the Chamber office underwent major renovations. In 1990 the Chamber wrote a resolution to support the building of a Civic Center. The Chamber formed a new committee to take a lead role in supporting the formation of the new Florence City-County Civic Center. A joint committee was formed in 1992 with the city and the Chamber to compile a long-range strategic report called Vision 2000.

In addition to responding to over 45,000 inquiries annually, the Chamber publishes a Membership Directory, newcomers guides, business pages, Directory of Civic Clubs and Organizations, and city-county maps.

The Greater Florence Chamber of Commerce played a lead role in supporting the formation of a Civic Center for the Pee Dee region. Pictured above is the groundbreaking ceremony of the Florence City-County Civic Center.

While all of this has been going on, the Chamber has grown in size. It now has over 850 firms as members with over 1,500 representatives. The budget has grown from $29,000 in 1960, to over $435,000 in 1995. At present, a staff of eight serves the membership. The Chamber is truly involved in promoting industrial, commercial, civic, and educational development of the area.

Waters-Powell Funeral Home

Waters-Powell Funeral Home, founded in 1893, has a history almost as long as that of the city of Florence. In July, 1893, Washington Marion Waters Sr. (1861-1939) opened a furniture store in the 100 block of South Dargan Street, which included the operation of the city's first funeral home. This followed an established pattern in which funeral homes were generally operated as an adjunct to furniture or hardware stores. At that time the chief service offered by funeral homes was the furnishing of a casket, and most caskets were handmade on demand.

Waters was a native of Goldsboro, North Carolina, and he came to Florence as an 18-year-old boy in 1879. His furniture store became one of the largest in eastern South Carolina, and he was nationally known as a mortician. Waters was elected mayor of Florence in 1923 and served until 1925. He served as Sunday school superintendent of the First Baptist Church from 1916 until his death, was a life deacon, and at the time of his death he was chairman of the board of deacons. A Rotarian, he served on the board of directors of the Florence YMCA.

In 1932 the furniture store operation was separated from the funeral home. The furniture store continued to be operated on South Dargan Street, and the Waters Funeral Home was moved to a residence at the corner of Pine and Dargan Streets. The residence was remodeled for use as a funeral home and featured, as an innovation, a convertible chapel with removable partitions so that it could be enlarged. In accordance with the prevalent custom, the funeral homes, as a community service, offered ambulance service during the period before the 1960s.

With the death of W. M. Waters Sr., the business was conducted by his sons, Joe Payne Waters (1904-52) and Cyril A. Waters (1896-1967). Joe Waters Sr. was born in Florence. After graduating from high school here, he was graduated from Furman University. He played football in both high school and college. He returned to Florence and was employed by various businesses before he assumed the managership of Waters Funeral Home in 1936. At the time of his death, he was a member of the board of deacons of the First Baptist Church and the board of directors of Connie Maxwell Orphanage.

Upon the death of Joe P. Waters, his son Joe P. Waters Jr. took over his interest in the operation of the business in conjunction with Cyril Waters. Cyril Waters was born in Florence, and after his early schooling was graduated from Bailey Military Institute in Greenwood, South Carolina, and attended the University of North Carolina. He served in the military in World War I, and among the many organizations in which he was active were Fred H. Sexton Post No. 1 of the American Legion, La Societe des 40 Hommes and 8 Chavaux, and the Veterans of Foreign Wars. Cyril Waters served on the Florence County Governing Board from 1933 to 1939. He was on the register of National Selected Morticians, South Carolina Funeral Directors Association, served as a board member of Florence Museum and James F. Byrnes Academy, and was a 10-year

W.M. Waters (1861-1939)

member on the board of deacons of the First Baptist Church.

A new funeral home was constructed on the site of the converted residence in 1964, which offers the most modern facilities for the conduct of funeral services. After the death of Cyril Waters, his nephew, Joe P. Waters Jr., operated the business. In 1982 Charles W. Powell purchased the funeral home from Joe P. Waters Jr. The name was changed to Waters-Powell Funeral Home in 1988.

Charles Powell was born in Dillon County, South Carolina, but he moved to Kingstree at an early age and was educated in the public schools there. In 1959 he moved to Florence and attended Francis Marion College when it was a branch of the University of South Carolina. That same year, Powell became an intern at Waters Funeral Home and lived in the funeral home. He was a nighttime ambulance driver who went out on ambulance calls to transport clients, whether living or deceased. This changed when EMS as a special service became available in the community. He was graduated from the Kentucky School of Mortuary Science in 1968 and returned to Waters Funeral Home, where he was employed as funeral director and embalmer. Powell has served as secretary of the South Carolina Funeral Directors Association and was president of that association in 1988. He served as a member of the South Carolina State Board of Funeral Service and was its president in 1978. Powell is a member of National Selected Morticians and National Funeral Directors Association, Florence Rotary Club, and Greenwood Baptist Church.

Powell operates the funeral home with the assistance of his son, Charles W. Powell Jr., who is a funeral director.

Charles W. Powell Sr.

Waters-Powell Funeral Home is the oldest service business which has been continually operating in the city of Florence. Powell states, with understanding, that "we provide special services that are needed during a very stressful period." Waters-Powell follows in that fine tradition established by its founder and his successors to provide quality, compassionate funeral services in the Pee Dee region.

BellSouth

BellSouth strives to exceed customer expectations...Shown above are BellSouth Associates and Florence Morning News Executives discussing features of the new equipment that BellSouth installed in the new Florence Morning News building on Dargan Street.

BellSouth, formerly known as Southern Bell, has served Florence since 1894–more than 100 years. In the beginning, there were 34 customers in Florence who had telephones–today there are almost 50,000. In 1894 all telephone calls were placed with the assistance of an operator. Direct local dialing was instituted in 1950, when there were 6,653 customers. Direct long-distance dialing was introduced in 1969. Florence was the "old Bell System's" first exchange to convert completely to electronic switching system technology on April 16, 1972, the date when Touch-Tone™ service became available.

Telecommunications technology has expanded at an ever increasing rate during the hundred years that BellSouth has grown with Florence. BellSouth's network is state-of-the-art and is 100-percent digital in Florence and the surrounding areas. E-911 is in place countywide, and advanced communications features such as TouchStar and MemoryCall are available for customers to enjoy. BellSouth's business customers are able to select from a wide array of products and services designed to make their businesses more efficient and profitable.

Florence is the home of BellSouth's Fleet Operations Center, which handles all of the administrative work for thousands of BellSouth vehicles across a nine-state area. Processing Clerk Wandell Burch helps keep the vehicles rolling.

Outstanding telecommunications service requires significant investment and foresight. The need for better and faster communications has resulted in huge capital investments by telephone companies across the nation, and BellSouth is no exception. At the end of 1995, BellSouth's network investment in South Carolina was valued at $2.6 billion dollars. That network includes virtually instantaneous transmission of voice, data, video, and facsimile signals through more than 107,000 miles of fiber-optic cable. With this new technology in place, calls go through faster, conversations are clearer, and data communications are more accurate.

The technology investment has also been made with reliability of service in mind. The ultimate opportunity for BellSouth's network to prove itself came when Hurricane Hugo blew across the Pee Dee region in September, 1989. People in the area suffered tremendous hardships, but most Florence residents found that their telephone service stayed intact. Underground cables, fiber optics, backup computer systems, and backup emergency power helped to keep communications flowing. BellSouth employees also played a critical role in keeping service activated for customers during this time. In addition to local employees, BellSouth asked many of its employees in other parts of its nine-state region to help in the Florence area.

Since the experience of Hurricane Hugo, reliability has been increased even more by BellSouth's installation of backup-fiber optic routes between many of its switching centers. This equipment allows BellSouth to route transmissions in another direction, if necessary, so that customers do not lose service if an underground cable is cut.

BellSouth knows that the health of the community is directly related to its success, and encourages employees to be active. The employees of BellSouth are actively involved in civic and religious organizations in their communities. The company helps support community organizations like United Way, the Pee Dee Education Foundation, and the Greater Florence Chamber of Commerce. The chairman of the board of the Florence Chamber for 1996-97 is William P. "Pat" Patton, manager of Corporate and External Affairs in BellSouth's Florence office. Many employees are a part of the company's community relations team, while others are involved in helping the BellSouth Telephone Pioneers with community projects designed to help the elderly, the handicapped, and others in need of assistance.

Lenair Thrower, electronics technician, completes a connection at the central switching office, and activates a customer's service.

The technology made possible through BellSouth's network has allowed the company to become more and more efficient over the years. Many internal functions, formerly done locally in Florence, are now done in centralized locations. Even though many functions have been consolidated and moved to other cities, one function has been centralized and brought to Florence, adding almost 60 jobs to the local economy. All of BellSouth's Fleet Operations administrative functions for its entire nine-state region are managed from Florence, South Carolina.

By comparison with the present, in the past the office and switchboard operations of BellSouth were conducted from an office on South Dargan Street, with female operators, in full view of passersby, personally handling calls. The familiar "Number, please" was the invitation to place a call. Many subscribers were on party lines, which meant waiting one's turn to place a call. In the 1928 Telephone Directory, there was an important, but somewhat mysterious, notice to party line subscribers. "If you are a party line subscriber and wish to call another party on your line, do not give the operator the complete number of the telephone wanted. Just say, 'I want to talk to J on this line,' or, M, R or W as the case may be, and then hang up the receiver while the operator rings the other telephone. When you think the party you are calling has had time to answer the telephone, remove your receiver and proceed with the conversation." James L. Duffell (1893-1963) was, for many years, the manager of the telephone office during that period.

From small beginnings in 1894 to state-of-the art technology and 50,000 customers today, BellSouth has grown with Florence. What does this mean to BellSouth customers?

Stability, service, innovation.

These children are fascinated by the electronic testing equipment used by Service Technician Clarence Hamilton.

"And it's also a smart investment," according to Patton, "for our customers and for BellSouth. The future of regional companies such as ours is directly linked to the prosperity of the individual communities that we serve."

"For over 100 years we have been proud to link our destiny to that of the Florence area, and we look forward to continuing to meet the telecommunications needs of all our customers through state-of-the-art technology," Patton added. "In fact, a new wireless service, known as PCS, is being introduced in the summer of 1996 as the latest breakthrough in telecommunications technology. But technology is not an end in itself. Our mission is to bring people and information together. By doing that, we enable our customers to do business and to share information with one another. That is good for everyone in our region and in our state."

Willcox, McLeod, Buyck & Williams

Willcox, McLeod, Buyck & Williams was founded in 1895 and is the oldest continuous law firm in northeastern South Carolina.

The original partners of the firm were Fred L. Willcox (1870-1937) and P. A. Willcox (1866-1922). From its earliest days, the lawyers of this firm engaged in a wide-ranging general law practice and participated in a wide variety of businesses and other successful endeavors across the region. Its members have been connected with most major economic and social advancements in the Pee Dee region from railroads, timber, and bright leaf tobacco to International Paper, the Florence Air Base, and the DuPont Company. Partners have included those who became state and federal judges, U. S. Attorneys, legislators, presidents of the South Carolina Bar Association and of the South Carolina Defense Trial Attorneys Association, trustees of the University of South Carolina and the State Technical Colleges, trustees of the major hospitals in Florence, and members of the boards of major corporations of the area.

Fred L. Willcox, 1870-1937

Its practice expanded on a business and litigation foundation, with particular emphasis on the defense of claims. The firm's practice has grown in geographic scope, now encompassing litigating cases in all of South Carolina's eastern counties and throughout the Federal Court system. The cases handled by the firm have diversified, encompassing insurance coverage questions and questions of products liability, business litigation, major casualty litigation, professional malpractice, real estate acquisition and development, foreclosure litigation, employment law, and general corporate law.

Some of the outstanding lawyers who have practiced with the firm, including the original partners, are Hugh L. Willcox (1904-94) and Hugh L. Willcox Jr., A. L. Hardee (1893-1969), Henry E. Davis (1879-1966), Melvin Purvis (1903-60), Stokes Houck (1898-1962) and his son, U. S. District Judge Weston Houck, W. Laurier O'Farrell (1913-79), the late South Carolina Supreme Court Chief Justice D. Gordon Baker (1884-1958) and his grandson, Gordon B. Baker Jr., Richard A. Palmer (1913-74), J. W. Wallace (1900-1971), James C. McLeod Jr., Mark W. Buyck Jr., Reynolds Williams, Mark W. Buyck III, Hunter Limbaugh, E. Lloyd Willcox II, Craig Young, Robert T. King, Brad T. Willbanks, and John H. Muench.

In celebration of its centennial, the firm published a history written by Roy Talbert Jr. entitled *No Greater Legacy,* which was highly acclaimed in the legal and historical communities. Talbert discusses the success of the firm and concludes that members of the firm today sit on a wide variety of community and corporate boards, continuing a legacy that began over a century ago. The story of the Willcox firm is part and parcel of the history of Florence, the Carolinas, and the New South.

The senior partners of the present firm. *Seated left to right:* Hugh L. Willcox Jr., Mark W. Buyck Jr., James C. McLeod Jr. *Standing:* Reynolds Williams.

Stoudenmire-Dowling Funeral Home

Ernest L. Oulla (1881-1960) acquired, in the early 1900s, a business long-remembered as "The Vaughan Undertaking Company." The new business was operated as Oulla's, Inc., and it was advertised as offering "Furniture and Pianos, Ambulance Service, Funeral Directors." The funeral home was located on South Dargan Street next door to St. John's Episcopal Church.

The McLeod House, circa 1917, is the site of Stoudenmire-Dowling Funeral Home.

Expansion became necessary as Mr. Oulla's clientele began to increase. The residence of Dr. Frank H. McLeod Sr. at 300 South Dargan Street became available. The McLeod house, which was completed in 1917, was one of the residential showplaces of Florence. A brick structure, it incorporated many elaborate architectural details and had been the family home of Dr. McLeod for nearly 20 years.

In the early 1930s the price of the McLeod residence was reported to be $10,000 dollars, a tremendous price at that time. In order to purchase the house, Oulla used the property on which his funeral home stood as a down payment. Oulla Funeral Home moved into the old McLeod home at the corner of Dargan and Palmetto Streets and has remained at that location ever since.

In 1946 Conner D. Stoudenmire (1911-86), who for many years had operated the Darlington Funeral Home in Darlington, South Carolina, purchased the Oulla Funeral Home from E. L. Oulla. In 1948 the name of the business was changed to Stoudenmire Funeral Home.

Stoudenmire saw the need for his funeral home to have a chapel to help better serve his client families. He wanted more than just a large room within the confines of the funeral home where chairs were set up for a funeral. He wanted his chapel to be unique, so in 1950 construction began on what was one of South Carolina's first freestanding funeral chapels. It had a church-like appearance and atmosphere with a high-pitched roof, a ceiling over 30 feet at its highest point, church pews, stained glass, and a private family room. Over the next several years, Stoudenmire was able to acquire adjoining properties to increase the size of his parking areas. Always upgrading and modernizing, he never allowed the original beauty and splendor of the McLeod home to be lost.

In 1973 Stoudenmire incorporated his business, allowing his employees to become stockholders. Two of them, Alton Parker and Merle Baxley, remained stockholders and active employees until their deaths.

In 1980 John F. Dowling joined the staff as a funeral director and embalmer. A native of Darlington County, Dowling had been associated as a stockholder with funeral homes in both Darlington and Hartsville. In early 1981, he was named manager of the firm and purchased a portion of the business. Upon the death of Stoudenmire in 1986, Charlotte C. Stoudenmire was named the president, and Dowling was named vice president and general manager. On June 30, 1988, Dowling purchased all of the outstanding stock in the corporation. Since that time, he has served as president and general manager, and his wife, Wanda Haynes Dowling, as vice president and office manager.

In 1990 the name of the corporation was changed to Stoudenmire-Dowling Funeral Home, Inc. In addition to the Dowlings, the business is staffed by Terry J. Burnham, Roger E. Poston, Harvey H. Woods, Chad O. Nettles, and Paul E. Elmore.

The Dowlings are proud of their funeral home and its rich heritage, and they are also proud to be a part of the Florence community.

In 1950 Conner Stoudenmire added this freestanding funeral chapel, one of the first in South Carolina.

McLeod Regional Medical Center

McLeod Regional Medical Center renders medical services of the highest order to Florence and the Pee Dee region. It is the largest employer in Florence County's private sector. Its progress represents the culmination of distinguished service by trustees, physicians, nurses, administrators, and employees which established a legacy of compassionate care and sustained McLeod Center as the region's leader in quality health care for nearly 100 years.

Dr. Frank Hilton McLeod Sr. (1868-1944) was the creator of that legacy. Born in Old Hundred, North Carolina, he attended Wofford college, Atlanta Medical School, and received his medical degree from the University of Tennessee in 1888, the year that Florence County was created. Dr. McLeod came to Florence to practice medicine in 1891 with Dr. Furman Payne Covington, the year after the city of Florence was incorporated.

McLeod Regional Medical Center has been a leader in providing quality health care for the Pee Dee region for nearly 100 years.

In 1900 there were 10 physicians in addition to Dr. McLeod practicing in Florence: Peter B. Bacote (1838-1924), Furman Payne Covington (1859-1918), James Evans (1831-1909), Benjamin B. Gregg (1873-1933), William Ilderton (1863-1918), John B. Jarrot, Lawrence Y. King (1869-1916), James R. Levy (1861-1936), and C. H. Prince. Dr. McLeod, realizing the need for surgical services in Florence, established the Florence Infirmary in 1906, in a remodeled residence on Cheves Street. A training school for nurses was started there almost immediately and continued until 1966. This was the beginning of McLeod Regional Medical Center.

Dr. McLeod became a statewide medical leader through his participation in an American College of Surgeons program designed to upgrade the quality of hospital care by establishing national standards. By 1921 the Florence Infirmary was the only hospital in the Pee Dee region and one of only three in South Carolina which met those standards. Using guidelines from the American College of Surgeons, Dr. McLeod began recruiting doctors with varying specialties. These specialists included Dr. Julian H. Price (1901-1990), pediatrics; Dr. James C. McLeod (1897-1947), surgery and gynecology; Dr. Orion T. Finklea (1895-1959), urology; Dr. Simons R. Lucas (1985-1946), ophthalmology; Dr. Marion R. "Dolph" Mobley (1890-1984), otolaryngology; Dr. Walter R. Mead (1897-1967), internal medicine; and Dr. Percy D. Hay (1899-1977), radiology.

During the 1920s, the Florence Infirmary operated as a successful proprietary institution. It had grown from a remodeled residence to a four-story building and was the third largest general hospital in the state, with facilities for radium treatment for cancer and an electrocardiography machine for diagnosing cardiac patients. Dr. McLeod, however, began seeking ways to make it a nonprofit operation to enhance its potential for growth as a community hospital. Eventually, he turned to the Duke Endowment, which made grants to nonprofit hospitals in North and South Carolina. With a grant of $125,000 from the Duke Endowment and a matching grant from Dr. McLeod, a self-perpetuating board of trustees was created and the name was changed to the McLeod Infirmary. The Infirmary was chartered on April 1, 1930, and it became a nonprofit community hospital.

F. H. McLeod, the man who inspired the legacy of excellence at McLeod Regional Medical Center.

The McLeod Infirmary continued to grow. To meet the need for expansion, the Public Works Administration granted, in 1932, a $300,000 loan for a new facility, and Duke Endowment donated

$35,000 for new equipment. The new seven-story building, located on Cheves Street between Dargan and Irby Streets, was occupied in 1935. It provided 200 beds and was generally recognized as the best built and equipped hospital in northeastern South Carolina. McLeod Infirmary retained its original mission of providing health care to all ages of people, supplying primary care in Florence and nearby communities, and serving as a referral hospital for residents of the Pee Dee region.

Dr. Frank McLeod retired in 1940, and the board of trustees named his son, Dr. James C. McLeod, superintendent of the hospital. Dr. James McLeod was born in Florence and attended Davidson College and the University of North Carolina. He received his medical degree from Cornell Medical School and interned at Bellevue Hospital in New York, specializing in Surgery. In 1924 he returned to Florence. He played a dominant role in securing the grants which made possible the building of the new McLeod Infirmary. Dr. James McLeod was a veteran of both World War 1 and II. He was active in civic life in Florence and served as president of the South Carolina Medical Association from 1946 to 1947. He was married to the former Floramay Holliday, and they had four children.

During World War II, there was a small medical unit attached to the Florence Army Air Base. The physicians stationed there were welcomed into the Florence County Medical Society and allowed privileges at McLeod Infirmary. Following World War II, great progress was made in medical research such as antibiotics and chemotherapy. The McLeod Infirmary was in the forefront in assimilating and initiating these advances in the Pee Dee.

***Standing:* Dr. F. H. McLeod, University of Tennessee Medical School, 1887**

After the death of Dr. James McLeod in 1947, the board of trustees took a more active part in the operation of the hospital. Finding funds to run the growing hospital and upgrading its physical plant took much of the board's time. While additions were made to the building during the 1950s, it was apparent that a larger building on a new site or major renovations were mandatory. Additional beds were sought through the purchase of the Florence-Darlington Tuberculosis Sanitorium in 1966. The negotiations leading to its purchase resulted in the addition of two trustees from Darlington County, making the board representative of a wider community. Plans to develop the sanitorium's facilities, however, were put on hold while the board continued to look at other alternatives.

One of the alternatives, aside from expanding the former Tuberculosis Sanitorium, was to construct "a large regional hospital to serve the Pee Dee Region." Its estimated cost was $20 to $30 million, with funding to come from private, state, and federal sources. This was not a new idea. In 1947 the South Carolina Board of Health had devised a hospital plan for the state in which it was divided into regions. The eight counties of the Pee Dee region, excluding Georgetown County, constituted one medical region. The city of Florence was recognized to be the center of the group of counties.

In 1968 a comprehensive analysis of South Carolina's health care services identified "natural regions" for health care delivery around Charleston, Columbia, Greenville, and Florence. The study noted that well-developed facilities existed in each of these cities except Florence and suggested that one was needed there. The board of trustees received a grant to pay for a study which would be a precise evaluation of the need for a medical center and the means of financing it. That study was released in July, 1971. It recommended the creation of a regional medical complex in Florence that would be a "center for patient care, education, clinical investigation, public health and community health activities." The report also recommended that an existing hospital, the McLeod Infirmary, be the

The McLeod Infirmary, 1910

nucleus of such a regional medical center instead of building a new hospital for that purpose. As part of the new imaging of McLeod Infirmary, the name was changed to McLeod Memorial Hospital.

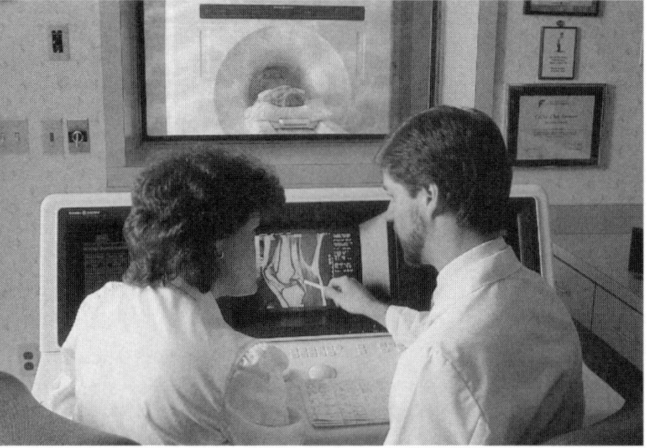

While steeped in history, McLeod Regional Medical Center continues to move forward with the highest levels of technology to facilitate patient care.

The concept of a regional medical center received a boost when the General Assembly passed an act in 1973 creating the Pee Dee Regional Health Services District comprised of Chesterfield, Darlington, Florence, Marlboro, Marion, and Dillon Counties. The 15-member board of this district was authorized to "plan, build, maintain, equip, and operate regional health care facilities or any other hospital or health care related facility" in the district.

However, the Health District was not able, on its own, to raise the funds necessary to build the regional health center. The McLeod Board assumed that responsibility. The county of Florence gave $1 million; the state gave over a half million; and the federal government gave substantial guaranties in interest and in subsidies. A fund-raising effort produced $3 million, of which $1 million came from the Duke Endowment.

A certificate of need for construction of a regional medical center was approved by the South Carolina Department of Health and Environmental Control in 1975. The name of the hospital was changed to McLeod Regional Medical Center of the Pee Dee that year. The number of members serving on the board was expanded to include representation from all of the counties which were included in the Health District.

A new site on which to build a regional medical center would be required. In 1979 the Housing Authority of Florence had acquired and cleared land in east Florence. On May 12, 1976, 30 acres of this land was conveyed to the city of Florence; the city deeded it to the Pee Dee Regional Health Services District; and the regional district leased it to the McLeod board for a term of 50 years with the right to renew for an additional 50 years. Construction was commenced on part of the 30 acres and ground was broken for the regional center in 1976, and the new facility was dedicated in September, 1979. Two months later the operation was moved there from the Cheves Street building, on November 16, 1979.

In 1974 McLeod Regional was recognized by Governor John C. West as the region's tertiary health provider. This empowered McLeod Center to provide the highest level of care for the most acutely ill patients in the Pee Dee region. Its primary care area has a population of 600,000, while its secondary service area has almost one million. Almost 50 percent of McLeod Medical Center's inpatients are from outside Florence County.

During the 1980s, the facilities were improved and enlarged. A neonatal intensive care unit was added; acute beds were arranged in six-bed pods to provide more privacy and better nursing efficiency; educational space was increased; and a Family Practice building, an Area Health Education Center building, and numerous classrooms and conference rooms in the main hospital were added. During the mid-1980s, a freestanding psychiatric unit with 35 beds was added; a medical unit of 31 beds was added; a center to provide Magnetic Resonance Imaging was opened in 1987; a program of open-heart surgery was begun in 1986; and new space for physical therapy, respiratory therapy, and radiation therapy was added. The McLeod Pediatric Department, established in 1929, was designated a Children's Hospital. It became a member of the national network of children's hospitals, which are involved in the annual Miracle Network Telethon, in 1986. That year, the McLeod Medical Center Foundation was formed to serve as a vehicle to attract donations to be used in organizing fund-raising projects. The monies raised are used to strengthen

Floramay Holliday McLeod, wife of Dr. James C. McLeod Sr.

programs of research, education, and service; to acquire technology; and to perpetuate medical excellence. The foundation continues to be the only charitable foundation whose mission is directed exclusively toward achieving excellence in health care in the Pee Dee region.

Dr. James Carlisle McLeod Sr., son of F. H. McLeod, became superintendent of the hospital in 1940 after his father's retirement.

Today, the McLeod Health System includes Wilson Medical Center in Darlington and McLeod Home Health, Inc., purchased in 1995, a leading provider of in-home care. Its structures include the Medical Center, the Women's Pavilion, and three physician office buildings. It also serves as the flagship facility for a network of 12 hospitals in the Palmetto Community Network, formed in 1994. This was the first regional partnership established in South Carolina to share resources and better coordinate health care.

The growth of McLeod Regional Medical Center has been phenomenal. In 1972 there were 63 physicians on the staff of McLeod Memorial Hospital, and in 1996 there are 230 physicians on the staff. In 1977 there were 750 people employed by the hospital, and in 1996 over 2,500 are employed. In 1977 McLeod Regional Medical Center rendered 67,000 patient days of care, while in 1995 there were 114,000 patient days of care. Surgical procedures increased from 6,900 in 1982, to 11,895 in 1995, including an average of more than 400 open-heart procedures performed annually since 1986. Deliveries increased from 1,800 in 1977 to nearly 3,000 annually by 1991. Emergency services visits increased from 1,800 in 1977 to more than 5,000 in 1995.

McLeod Regional Medical Center has been fortunate in the directors which it has had since 1977. In April, 1977, while the new building was under construction, Charles H. Frenzel (1919-93), former director of Duke University Medical Center, was appointed president of McLeod Regional Medical Center. He served as president until 1984. J. Bruce Barragan, formerly the executive vice president of the medical center, succeeded Frenzel as president on January 1, 1985, and continues to serve as president today. Chairmen of the board of trustees since 1930, and the dates of their chairmanships, are as follows: Joseph C. Long (1930-34), Benjamin W. Covington (1934-47), Ranson B. Hare (1947-59), Marshall L. "Jack" Meadors (1959-75), J. Givens Young (1975-82), and D. Laurence McIntosh (1982-present).

McLeod Regional Medical Center provides high quality, high-tech and state-of-the-art medical services through its varied Centers of Excellence, which include The McLeod Heart Institute, the McLeod Cancer Center for Treatment and Research, the McLeod Children's Hospital, the McLeod Women's Pavilion, Greenland Park Behavioral Health Sciences Center, the McLeod Emergency Services, Radiological Services, Neurosciences, and Surgery Center. Improving the health of the region's citizens remains the number one priority of McLeod Regional Medical Center as a new century approaches. Its legacy of excellence is based on the dedication of its doctors, nurses, trustees, administrators, employees, and volunteers. People are McLeod's most valuable resource, and McLeod Regional Medical Center will continue to advance, investing in recruitment, retention, education, and training to ensure that as medical knowledge grows, so will its delivery of health care to the people of the Pee Dee region.

Improving the health of the region's citizens remains the number one priority of McLeod Regional Medical Center.

Aiken & Company

The history of Aiken & Company began in 1914 when Jefferson Boone Aiken Sr. (1889-1978) came to Florence as the general agent in the Pee Dee region of the old Southeastern Life Insurance Company. He was married to Pearl Ellis (1889-1968), a Florence native and daughter of Osborn S. Ellis (1856-1917), a pioneer citizen. His first business partner was J. C. "Joe" Long, and the business went by the name Aiken & Long. In 1924 Aiken sold the life insurance business to Long and kept the fire, casualty, and bond business, taking the name Aiken & Company. The company has been doing business under that name since then.

Over the years, Aiken's involvement in the community was deep and varied. He organized the Florence Rotary Club and was its first president in 1921. He served as a district governor of Rotary in 1932, when the district was the entire state of South Carolina and half of North Carolina. In 1933 Dr. Frank H. McLeod asked Aiken to be one of the original trustees, with life tenure, of the newly completed McLeod Infirmary on Cheves Street.

The Federal Housing Administration was created in 1934. However, it did little business until the government created a secondary market for FHA home mortgages in 1938 by establishing the Federal National Mortgage Association (FNMA). This enabled FHA-approved mortgage companies to sell their mortgages to FNMA, retain servicing, and repeat the process, thus continuously building the servicing volume. Aiken saw the opportunity this presented and immediately organized the Aiken Loan & Security Company to originate and service mortgages.

By 1939 two of Boone Aiken's sons, Osborn S. and Jefferson B. Jr., and a son-in-law, David H. McLeod (1915-86), were working in the combined Aiken & Company/Aiken Loan & Security Company. During World War II, the business marked time. O.S. and J.B. Jr. served in the Navy, and a younger son, John D. "Jack" Aiken, withdrew from the Citadel in 1943 and served in the Air Force. By 1946 the two older sons had rejoined the family business, and later Jack became linked with it on a special assignment basis.

J. Boone Aiken, founder of Aiken & Company

Jefferson B. Aiken Jr.

The year 1950 was a major milestone in Boone Aiken's career. That year he and his closest associate, John G. "Doc" Hyman (1894-1965), bought a major interest in the Guaranty Bank & Trust Company, a local bank that had been organized in 1936. This did two things. It gave Aiken something to which he could devote his creative business acumen, and it made room at Aiken & Company/Aiken Loan & Security Company for his sons and son-in-law to apply more of their time and effort to the business and to community service.

Boone's imprimatur on the Guaranty Bank was to project it as the Home Town Bank. His messages to the public were expressed in these themes: "Dollar profit is not first at the Home Town Bank," and "We strive to run the kind of bank you want to do business with regardless of the FDIC insurance… (which, incidentally, we do provide)."

During this new period, David McLeod served as mayor of Florence for 16 years, from 1954 to 1970. His administration was highlighted by Florence's being named an "All-America City," and by attracting to Florence its first national industry, the DuPont Company.

During this same period of time, O. S. Aiken served on the Florence District I School Board from 1952 to 1972. He served as chairman for the last 16 of those years and helped to recruit as superintendent, Henry Sneed.

J.B. Jr. worked mainly at the mortgage company and expanded its growth with branch offices in Columbia, Greenville, and Charleston in South Carolina; Raeford, North Carolina; and Thomson, Georgia. He also set up Construction Advance Corporation to lend construction money to builders to create permanent loans for the mortgage servicing company. The financing was done with banks other than the Guaranty.

James M. Harsh

While the mortgage company was sold in 1972, the subsequent owners have left the servicing in Florence. The large Fleet Funding Servicing Center on Evans Street employs hundreds of people and is the continuation of that part of the operation started in Florence in 1938.

In other community service, David McLeod became a life trustee of McLeod Hospital. J.B. Jr. was elected a director of the *Florence Morning News* following the death of Mr. John M. O'Dowd in 1970, and as a trustee of McLeod Hospital following the death of his father in 1978.

Yesterday, Aiken & Company was essentially a family business. Today, it is a business family employing a team of highly trained, seasoned, and dedicated professionals. Its primary mission is insurance. It conducts a comprehensive operation in fire, casualty, bonds, life, health, and all types of insurance. Throughout its history it has given support and vitality to the independent insurance agency system and has a roster of strong, impressive companies with which to place its customers' insurance needs. Aiken & Company also serves the public in real estate sales and property management.

Its operation is highly computerized, and officers and customer service representatives have computer terminals allowing instant communication with its insurance companies and immediate access to every customer's account. The state-of-the-art computer system, updated in January of 1996, gives Aiken & Company the ability to do in-house rating as well as develop individualized proposals.

Aiken & Company's growth in recent years has been augmented by the acquisition of several other local independent agencies. In 1972 Aiken & Company purchased the Stevenson-Hyman Insurance Agency, which had been in business since 1908. In 1980 it purchased the Wallace H. Berger Agency, and in 1995 Aiken & Company acquired the Delta Insurance Agency.

Lynn R. Owens

Officer responsibility for the company is as follows:

- Henry C. Lentz, chairman
- Lynn R. Owens, president & chief executive officer
- James (Jim) M. Harsh, executive vice president
- Richard (Dickie) H. Reynolds, vice president, Life & Health Insurance
- Robert (Bobby) H. Streett, vice president, Real Estate & Property Management
- Dianne S. Street, assistant secretary

This brief recital of some of the history of Aiken & Company leaves unmentioned the contributions of many wonderful men and women who were a part of building and expanding the company. They are remembered with love, affection, and appreciation.

Carolinas Hospital System

As the largest hospital system in northeastern South Carolina, Carolinas Hospital System provides a comprehensive continuum of integrated health care services. With a dynamic vision for the future of health care in the region, the hospital continues to develop and enhance services dedicated to promoting the quality of life of the community and bolstering Florence's development as a major medical center in South Carolina.

On January 1, 1994, Carolinas Hospital System was formed from the consolidation of two medical organizations which were integral parts of the rich medical history of the Florence community. Florence General Hospital (founded in 1921) and Bruce Hospital System (founded in 1944) made notable contributions to the quality of life of citizens throughout the Pee Dee

Carolinas Hospital System-Cedar Tower, 1996

region. Their record of service will forever be a testament to the spirit of human kindness and caring which has provided the best medical care available. The histories of these two institutions record a deep, abiding love of medicine and a compassionate spirit, which were the guiding forces of that record of service.

It may seem ironic that in the year 1921, in the small southern town of Florence, it was a Northerner who founded the city's second hospital. Florence General Hospital opened on June 1st of that year under the name of Saunders Memorial Hospital. It was a 40-bed facility built by Dr. John Smyser, a native of New Jersey who completed graduate work at Johns Hopkins Medical School. While serving as an intern there, Dr. Smyser met and fell in love with one of his patients–Janie Sue Saunders of Florence. After marrying, the couple settled in Florence, where Dr. Smyser began practicing medicine.

At the outbreak of World War I, he was commissioned and called to active duty. While serving his country abroad, Dr. Smyser's father-in-law died. Following his tour of duty, Dr. Smyser returned to Florence, and with a grant of money bequeathed to him by his father-in-law, he established Saunders Memorial Hospital in his honor. The hospital was a brick structure located on Dargan Street on the site now

Carolinas Hospital System-Irby Tower, 1996

occupied by Professional Center Four of Carolinas Hospital System.

The hospital grew steadily, with a medical staff of six physicians. In 1929 the entire hospital was remodeled, giving it a colonial facade which many native Florentines still recall today. With a sweeping porch and grand, columned entrance, the hospital provided a warm welcome to all persons it served.

Following Dr. Smyser's death, his estate sold the hospital to Drs. Lamar Lee Sr. and Frank B. Lee Sr., nephews of Dr. John Barnwell, one of the original six physicians to serve at Saunders Memorial Hospital. In 1954 all of the hospital property was donated to the Saunders Memorial Hospital and Clinic Corporation, a private, nonprofit corporation.

During this era, life in Florence centered primarily in the downtown area, where retail stores, the courthouse, and movie theaters were located. People from all walks of life would gather at drug store fountains to enjoy cokes, ice cream floats, and homemade sandwiches. In stark contrast, the Five Points area that we know today as the bustling center of town was a quiet farming area.

Some years earlier, Dr. John Larrabee Bruce had traveled to Florence to serve an internship at Saunders Memorial Hospital. A native of St. Matthews, South Carolina, Dr. Bruce graduated from Wofford College and the South Carolina Medical College. After completing his internship, he remained in town practicing as a physician and surgeon, and subsequently, in 1944, he founded Bruce Hospital as a four-bed clinic in a residence on Dargan Street directly across from Saunders Memorial Hospital.

Only two years later, as a result of the need for expanded services, Bruce Hospital was incorporated as a nonprofit institution and undertook a great remodeling and expansion project that increased the number of beds and changed the appearance of the hospital, which had a new stucco facade.

At this time, Dr. Bruce began performing surgical procedures in the hospital. He had an elevator installed which opened directly into the operating room located on the second floor of the house. In fact, from there Dr. Bruce and others could enjoy watching the football games, practices, and other activities taking place on the athletic field behind the old Florence High School, later named McClenaghan High School, which adjoined Bruce Hospital on the corner of Dargan and Elm Streets.

In the early 1950s, Bruce Hospital purchased neighboring properties stretching to Cedar Street and added further to the original structure. Over a period of time, construction brought the main hospital building to the corner of Dargan and Cedar Streets. In three additional phases of expansion, facilities were added behind the main hospital down Cedar Street that would result in the present configuration of the hospital.

Saunders Memorial Hospital was also experiencing major growth during the decade of the 1950s. In 1957, new construction expanded the hospital facilities, assuring every patient a private room. Ten years later, a six-story tower was constructed which stands today as the east wing of the hospital. At the same time, the original building facing Dargan Street was leveled due to irreparable structural damage. The main entrance to the hospital now faced Irby Street, one of Florence's most heavily traveled roadways.

To better reflect the hospital's mission of service to the community, the board of trustees renamed the facility Florence General Hospital in 1972. A few years later, a seven-story tower was built as a west wing to the hospital.

Furthered by strong community support, Bruce Hospital continued to grow rapidly as well. On May 6, 1980, a groundbreaking ceremony was held for a new structure which would house the primary services of Bruce Hospital. Dr. Bruce, however, did not live to see the fulfillment of his dream. He died in 1979, two years before the new hospital opened with three floors. The fourth and fifth floors were completed in 1987.

Bruce Hospital, circa 1962

Bruce Hospital added a physical therapy department in 1977, the first hospital-affiliated PT department in Florence, and eventually a Work-Hardening Program which focused on returning injured employees to work. This eventually led to the development of a pioneering program where the hospital worked with local business and industry leaders to implement comprehensive, cost-effective medical and wellness programs to ensure a healthier, more viable workforce.

First of its kind in the Pee Dee region, this highly successful outreach service continues today through the Occupational Health Center of Carolinas Hospital System, where a trained staff works with more than 200 local businesses and industries to provide important health services.

Saunders Memorial Hospital, circa 1939

During the 1980s and early into the 1990s, both Florence General Hospital and Bruce Hospital System experienced unparalleled growth. Each contributed greatly to advancing many health care services in the community. Chief among these were laser surgery, cardiac and pulmonary rehabilitation, the region's first seizure laboratory, treatment for sleep disorders, outpatient surgery, adult day care, treatment for alcohol and drug dependency, and the area's first diabetes facility certified by the American Diabetes Association.

As these developments in medical care were being introduced to the Florence community, the administration of Bruce Hospital recognized that the hospital of the future must not only provide care for the sick, but should also provide health education and related services to help people maintain good health. Thus, an era of "wellness" was born in the Florence area. Bruce Hospital began an intensive effort to bring to the community an array of services that would complement the hospital's new mission of total health care, and a name change ensued. Bruce Hospital System better reflected this new dimension of the hospital's philosophy.

In order to carry forward this mission, additional physical plant was needed. Thus, in early 1982, the board of trustees authorized the purchase of the old McClenaghan High School and its renovation into a fitness and retirement center. In the meantime, work was proceeding on a complex of physicians' offices, known as Medical Plaza, on the site of the original Bruce Hospital. Today, these facilities comprise Professional Centers One, Two, and Three of Carolinas Hospital System.

On May 1, 1984, the Fitness Forum opened in the renovated McClenaghan High School as the first hospital-based wellness center in South Carolina. The retirement center, McClenaghan Place, opened in January 1985.

Just as these services ushered in a new focus on wellness, in 1989 new ground was broken in the delivery of health care to the community when the boards of trustees of Florence General Hospital and Bruce Hospital System took the first step toward an eventual partnership. That year, they voted to organize a joint venture that would offer specialized services at a more reasonable and justifiable cost to the community. These services included magnetic resonance imaging, cardiac catheterization, rehabilitation services, and maternity services through The Women's Center, a 20-bed freestanding hospital.

The success of this joint venture led to the consolidation of the two hospitals on January 1, 1994 as Carolinas Hospital System, creating the largest hospital system in the region with 424 licensed beds. The following year marked another important milestone in the hospital's organization when the board of trustees voted to sell the hospital to Nashville-based Quorum Health Group, Inc. The hospital became aligned with a national health care organization which provides expertise and access to greater resources, enabling Carolinas Hospital System to expand and broaden services offered to the community.

An ambulance waits outside the original building of Saunders Memorial Hospital, circa 1923

Left to right: **Dr. Leonard Ravenell, Dr. John Smyser, Dr. John Barnwell, Dr. Boykin**

The changes and growth witnessed during the year subsequent to the hospital's sale were dramatic, with improved diagnostic capabilities rivaling technology available at leading medical centers, and enhanced services such as neonatology and emergency care delivered in renovated, specially designed units. Such growth reflected the overall quality of medical care available in Florence and contributed not only to the growing stature of Florence as the medical hub for the Pee Dee region, but to its overall economic growth as well.

Carolinas Hospital System remains at the forefront of delivering quality medical care responsive to the growing needs of the community. Noting the sweeping changes the medical community has undergone since Saunders Memorial Hospital and Bruce Hospital were founded, and recognizing the continued dramatic change looming on the horizon for the delivery of medical care, Carolinas Hospital System today has a vision to enhance the quality of life for all the region's citizens with the construction of a new state-of-the-art hospital designed for the twenty-first century. Planned in conjunction with members of the local medical and business communities, the futuristic design will incorporate an integrated delivery system revolving around physician offices, diagnostic services and inpatient care. The facility will be unsurpassed in the region, introducing area residents to a new era in health care. Expected to be completed in 1998, it will embrace patient-focused care as a blueprint for the continued tradition of service that is a hallmark of Carolinas Hospital System.

Recognizing the need to reach beyond the hospital walls to effect the best health care delivery system possible, Carolinas Hospital System has also started developing regional network affiliations to enhance access to health care in different communities. These affiliations include partnerships with leading medical centers to provide highly specialized services such as perinatal care, as well as affiliations with community providers such as Lake City Community Hospital and multiple physician practices across the region. It also includes a dedicated outreach effort to bring services to communities, such as prenatal care, in order to nurture its commitment to better health into the future.

What is common today in medical care was most likely unthinkable in 1921. To know that babies born eight weeks premature could survive with minor complications...that tumors no larger than a seed could be detected and treated...or that doctors could probe the vessels of the heart to cure heart disease... all these are works of progress.

As Carolinas Hospital System continues to grow and expand, it will remain dynamic and progressive, committed to adding services dedicated solely to meeting the needs of the people in the Pee Dee region today, tomorrow, and into the next century. ♣

Dr. John L. Bruce

ATKINSON
SSGT
US AIR FORCE
WORLD WAR II
KOREA
MARLAND D
THOMAS BROGDON

Florence Morning News, Inc.

Florence Morning News, Inc. was purchased December 11, 1981, by Thomson Newspapers, Inc., a worldwide marketing and communications company. It became the owner of a newspaper which had influenced events in and contributed to the progress of the city of Florence and the Pee Dee region. The first edition of that newspaper, the *Weekly News Review,* appeared on March 18, 1922. Its immediate predecessor was the *Florence News and Review,* and its name was later changed to *Morning News Review.* In February, 1928, it purchased the *Florence Daily Times,* its competitor, and the name was changed to *Florence Morning News.*

The newspaper was owned jointly by John A. Zeigler (1888-1960), who served as editor, and James Ben Parnell (1887-1966), a printer who was its business manager. It first operated in a second-floor office over Zeigler's drug store at the corner of South Dargan and Evans Streets. The operation moved to a building on East Evans Street in 1928. John Michael O'Dowd (1887-1970) became a third owner of the business in 1923. He gradually took over the interests of Zeigler and Parnell and became sole owner in 1947, and remained its publisher until his death in 1970. After his death, the newspaper was published by a committee, which was replaced by a board of directors that oversaw the paper's operations until it was sold to Thomson Newspapers. Richard Moisio served as publisher until the sale.

From 1947 until October 1995, the Florence Morning News was located on South Irby Street.

John M. O'Dowd, a native of Orangeburg County, South Carolina, came to the newspaper business by a circuitous route. He was a bookkeeper for Southern Bell Telephone Company; a movie theater operator in 1909; and in 1911, when he moved to Florence, the lessor of the City Hall's Opera House on Evans Street, where he operated a movie theater. O'Dowd built his own movie theater, "O'Dowd Theater," on South Dargan Street and entered the newspaper business without prior experience.

There have been a number of editors of the *Florence Morning News.*

Mason C. Brunson (1878-1950) was editor in 1928, succeeding Zeigler. Brunson remained editor until 1947, and was succeeded by James Alton Rogers (1905-90). In 1947 the newspaper's operations moved to a building on South Irby Street and remained there until it moved to its present location on South Dargan Street in October, 1995. Rogers resigned in 1951 and was succeeded by Howard Leveque, who was succeeded in 1953 by John "Jack" Howard O'Dowd (1926-86), the publisher's adopted son. Jack O'Dowd, because of his unpopularity as editor during the integration crisis, was asked by his father to resign in 1956.

James Rogers returned as editor in 1956 and remained editor until 1975. Succeeding Rogers as managing editors for the years indicated were Joe B. Rickenbaker (1966-81), Thom Anderson (1981-86), Don Gordon (1986-89), and Darren Drevik (1989-92). The present editor is Frank Sayles Jr.

Currently, from the newspaper's Dargan Street location, the *Florence Morning News* has a circulation of 33,000 daily and 35,500 on Sundays.

There have been three publishers of the newspaper since Thomson purchased it–Tenny Griffin, 1981-85; John E. Miller, 1986-95; and C. Thomas Marschel, the present publisher.

The circulation of the *Morning News* is 33,000 daily and 35,500 on Sundays. Thomson Newspapers' Florence facility does the printing for several of the area's weekly newspapers. The newspaper has a nearly 100-year-old record of continuous public service in the Pee Dee region.

Sexton Dental Clinic

Sexton Dental Clinic has achieved national and international recognition for offering the best available dentures at the lowest price. The clinic has developed a system which allows a patient to have extractions and to be fitted with dentures within a 24-hour period. It is understood that the immediate dentures which are fitted in this manner are temporary and will, as a matter of course, have to be replaced by permanent dentures later.

Sexton Dental Clinic

Dr. Claude L. Sexton was the founder of the clinic. He was born on August 29, 1899, in Lillington, North Carolina, and graduated from the Dental School of Emory University in 1924. He was married to Katheryn Melvin in 1927, and established himself in the practice of dentistry in Florence shortly thereafter. It was his idea to focus the practice of dentistry on one service, the fabrication and fitting of dentures. All of the activities necessary for that service were concentrated in one location. This included the extraction of teeth, making of impressions, the manufacture of the dentures, and the fitting of the dentures. A one-day service operation became a reality, and with it, a greatly reduced price to the patient. Its appeal, besides the low cost, is the fact that the person having extractions will not have the inconvenience and disfigurement of being without dentures while waiting for the healing process.

Dr. Sexton was deeply involved in community life in Florence. He was a member of Central Methodist Church, where he served as chairman of its board of education and a member and chairman of its board of stewards. He donated the land on which Central Methodist Church built a camp near Florence, which was named Camp Sexton in his honor. He was a member and past president of the Florence Kiwanis Club and a former Lieutenant Governor of District 8, Kiwanis International. Other organizations in which Dr. Sexton took an active part were the Pee Dee Shrine Club and the Florence Elks Club.

Dr. Sexton took a keen interest in horses and livestock. He maintained a large farm in Tennessee for the breeding and training of Tennessee walking horses, and was a member of the Tennessee Walking Horse Breeder Association. He was also a life member of the American Angus Association.

He died on April 28, 1975. He had one daughter, Mrs. Dennis H. Williams (Betty) of Fayetteville, North Carolina. One of his four grandchildren, Lee Williams, is active in the Sexton Dental Clinic today.

There are approximately 80 persons employed by the clinic, and it is capable of treating as many as 250 patients a day. On any given day in the parking lots adjoining the clinic there may be cars with license plates from Arizona, Texas, New York, New Jersey, Ohio, and Connecticut. In fact, the clinic has, through the years, established a reputation that has brought patients from all over the nation and Canada to Florence. The reputation for value and quality have made the clinic's growth possible without extensive advertising.

The Sexton Dental Clinic has been the subject of numerous articles in newspapers and magazines which have emphasized the public service aspect of the clinic's operations. The story of the clinic has also been the subject of numerous specials on television. The regime which is followed by the clinic is not an easy one. It requires that its dentists and employees commence operations at 3:30 A.M. and continue into the afternoon until the work is finished.

Although there have been jokes made about the clinic's operation, such as calling Florence "the Tooth Capital of the World," none have suggested that the fundamental premise on which the clinic operates is false. It offers dental service to people of low income

Dr. Claude L. Sexton, founder of Sexton Dental Clinic

who, without the clinic, would have no dental care because of its expense.

There have been numerous Florence dentists who have been associated with the Sexton Dental Clinic. Service in the Sexton Dental Clinic has motivated other dentists to open similar clinics, but none has achieved its status.

When Dr. Sexton died, the leadership and control of the Sexton Dental Clinic was assumed by Dr. Hoyt Lefond Eagerton Jr. Dr. Eagerton was born on June 22, 1933, in Florence, South Carolina. His parents were the late Inez Andrews and Hoyt Lefond Eagerton Sr. He attended McClenaghan High School in Florence, and upon graduation, worked for two years for the Atlantic Coast Line Railroad. He was drafted into the Army and sent to Fort Eustis, Virginia, where he served for two years. He was transferred to Fort Sam Houston, San Antonio, Texas, and served on the staff of General Clooney.

After his discharge from the Army, he attended the University of South Carolina and graduated with a B.S. degree. In 1959 he enrolled in dental school at the University of Tennessee in Memphis, where he received a D.D.S. degree. He was first employed by the North Carolina Public Health Department as a school dentist. His primary duties were to practice and teach dental care to indigent children. He also practiced general dentistry in the Appalachian region of North Carolina.

In 1964, after passing the South Carolina Dental Boards, he became a member of the staff at Sexton Dental Clinic. Following the death of Dr. Sexton, he purchased the clinic from the Sexton estate and has practiced dentistry in Florence and directed the clinic since that time. He is a member of First Baptist Church and has two daughters–Lisa Ann Eagerton Jordan and Leigh Carol Eagerton.

In addition to specializing in the manufacture and fitting of immediate dentures, the clinic also does crowns, bridges, and restorative dentistry. Presently the clinic employs 10 dentists, 2 oral surgeons, and 85 technicians and dental assistants. The clinic opened a branch in Myrtle Beach, South Carolina, in 1981. The Myrtle Beach office is capable of seeing 100 patients a day.

While the primary purpose of Sexton Dental Clinic is to provide good, low-cost dental care to its patients, the impact of its operation in Florence should be noted. The Chamber of Commerce has estimated that the operation of Sexton Dental Clinic and others, which have begun a similar operation, generate between 8 to 10 million dollars annually in income for other businesses in the city of Florence through monies spent on motels, food, drugs, and other products and services.

Dr. Hoyt L. Eagerton Jr., current owner of Sexton Dental Clinic

County of Florence

Florence County has taken a lead in encouraging industry to locate in this county. As early as 1954, Florence County played a leading and crucial role in persuading Wellman, Inc. to locate in the Johnsonville area. With approximately 1,900 employees,

The Florence County Seal

Wellman is now the second largest employer in the county. Its location in the county in the 1960s was a portent of things to come.

The state's constitutions prior to the constitution of 1976 gave little power to counties. It was the accepted practice that all annual appropriations for county purposes had to be approved annually by the state legislature. The customary practice was established that only legislators for the county whose appropriations were being debated spoke and voted on its passage. This meant, in effect, that the legislative delegation, as the holder of the purse strings, had the final power to approve or disapprove appropriations for county purposes.

Further complicating the situation was the absence of any broad power of the county governing board to do any of the acts which a municipal corporation normally would be expected to perform. There is a tortuous history of legislative acts setting up county governing boards. In 1894 the legislature created the office of County Supervisor, who was to be elected by popular vote for a term of two years. In the words of the statute, he was given "General Jurisdiction over all public highways, roads, bridges, and ferries, over paupers, and in all matters relating to taxes and disbursement of public funds for county purposes." To advise the Supervisor, there was created a County Board of Supervisors, which consisted of the Supervisor and two, later three, appointed commissioners.

In 1922 the County Board of Supervisors was abolished and a body named the Past Indebtedness and Governing Commission, consisting of five members, was created. In 1924 the office of supervisor was abolished and a Governing Commission consisting of six members appointed by the governor and the foreman of the grand jury was created. In 1926 the commissioners were required to be nominated in the Democratic Party primary to be eligible for appointment, and in 1932 the Governing Commission was abolished and the Governing Board of Florence County was created. The requirement that the members of the Governing Board be nominated in the Democratic primary was abolished in 1944, and the new law required that they be nominated by the legislative delegation. This act also created the office of County Manager, but unlike the Supervisor, he was not given any powers other than administrative, and he was not a member of the Governing Board. The Home Rule Act of 1974 made the Governing Board of the County a municipal corporation for the first time.

The Florence County Council, consisting of nine members with a full-time county administrator, has brought county government into the twentieth century and is ready to carry it forward into the twenty-first century. Attracting industry has become such a major function of county government that an Economic Development Authority was created for that purpose. This has led to the creation of two industrial parks in the county with large tracts set aside for industry's future needs. The Economic Development Authority has become a driving force behind the county's future as it strives to make Florence County attractive to the world of business.

Members of the Florence County Council *(Left to right):* K. G. Rusty Smith Jr.; Russell W. Culberson; Joe W. King; J. L. Dinky Miles, vice chairman; Herbert F. Ames, chairman; John A. Hyman, secretary/chaplain; Mitchell Kirby, Waymon Mumford, Terry Alexander

Belk

The first Belk store was originally incorporated in 1897 by William Henry Belk (1863-1952), a native of Monroe, North Carolina. In 1934 Robert T. Riley (1899-1973) was given the opportunity by William Henry Belk Sr. to open the first Belk store in Florence, South Carolina. He was offered a partnership and allowed to buy stock in the company. With Mr. Belk's help, Riley found a vacant store building in downtown Florence. The building, located on the southeast corner of Evans and Dargan Streets, was the oldest building in Florence. It was built in 1867 by John Kuker and Julius Hoffmeyer, both immigrants from Germany. The ground floor was used for the mercantile business of Hoffmeyer & Kuker, and the top story was the residence of John Kuker and his family. The heirs of John Kuker sold the property to Belk Department Store, but the old building, 50' x 110', needed extensive repairs. It was determined that the walls were in a safe condition, and in March, 1935, the new company opened for business in one of Florence's landmarks.

This was the time of 6-cent cotton and 12-cent tobacco, and the community's purchasing power was dependent on agriculture and the railroads. The only industry of any size other than the Atlantic Coast Line Railroad was the American Bakeries, which employed 145 people. The nearest Belk store was in Bennettsville, 40 miles away.

Bob Riley worked for Henry Simpson in Greenville for three years and had learned many successful methods which he utilized in upgrading the Florence store's lines of merchandise as general business conditions improved. Riley was aided by the Charlotte offices, and his buyers worked closely with Belk Stores Services to build greater depth in all lines. However, growth created space problems.

An adjacent hardware store on East Evans Street was purchased in 1946. This increased the store's size to 80' x 110' and permitted moving men's and boys' merchandise into the new area, and using the second floor for women's and children's wear. Again in 1950, the store was remodeled when an additional 40 feet was added to the rear of the building, and an elevator, air-conditioning, and open-front display windows were installed.

The success of Belk's Florence store far exceeded expectations. Building on the Florence achievement, new stores were opened at Lake City (1948) and Kingstree (1949). In 1965 the downtown store was closed and Belk opened in the newly constructed Florence Mall. In 1980 Belk moved to its present location in Magnolia Mall, in a 139,000-square-foot building.

Bob Riley always acknowledged that people were the motivating force behind his store's success story—people like James T. Rice, assistant manager for many years until he retired in 1960 due to poor health, and Daniel P. Thompson, better known as "Tilly," who worked in the store during his high school days, then started full time in display, advertising, and many other jobs until he succeeded Mr. Rice as assistant manager. In 1965 Thompson was named manager of the new store at Florence Mall.

Upon Bob Riley's death in 1973, Thompson assumed the responsibility as partner of this group of stores. He supervises the Florence and Lake City stores, both successful, modern, fashionable, and leaders in their communities. Mr. Riley's widow, Matrice Phillips Riley, and their son, Robert T. Riley Jr., remain active as directors and stockholders of the stores.

Advertising "Gifts for All" in its early days, today's Belk is "All for You."

The Florence County Courthouse was extensively remodeled in 1935 with the help of WPA funding. Watercolor by Jane Jackson.

Pepsi Cola Bottling Company of Florence

The Pepsi Cola Bottling Company of Florence was started in 1936 by three men: A. R. Avent, William E. "Bill" Carpenter, and Thomas G. Bagwell. Its success story typifies the spirit of enterprise which Florence and the Pee Dee region nurtured.

Pepsi Cola originated during the Depression. In 1933 Joseph Lapides, a flavor bottler in the Baltimore, Maryland, area, bottled Pepsi Cola in a 12-ounce bottle and marketed it, claiming it gave "twice as much for a nickel." It was a success, and Lapides began arranging for franchises along the eastern seaboard.

Avent had managed a soft drink bottling company in Wadesboro, North Carolina, but decided to go into business for himself. He negotiated a franchise agreement which covered the nine counties of the Pee Dee region, moved to Florence, bought used machinery which he had shipped there, rented and adapted a building on North Dargan Street, bought two delivery trucks, and Pepsi Cola Bottling Company of Florence was chartered. Avent held 52 percent of the stock, Carpenter 31 percent, and Bagwell 17 percent. The company produced the first case of Pepsi Cola for sale in March, 1936.

Avent realized that the building and machinery were inadequate for a growing business. A lot was purchased on South Irby Street, a building was constructed on the lot, new machinery was installed, and the operation moved early in 1938.

Pepsi Cola Bottling Company of Florence, c. 1939, on South Irby Street

After Carpenter's death, in 1947 the Conway territory was severed and given to Carpenter's family as their share of the corporate assets.

In 1948 a bottling plant was built in Bennettsville. T. G. Bagwell took this plant and the Bennettsville territory as his share of the corporate assets. This decision to separate the Bennettsville territory made Avent and his family the sole owners of the corporation. The remaining territory included all of Florence, Darlington, Dillon, and Williamsburg Counties, the greater part of Georgetown County, and a portion of Marlboro County.

Between 1950 and 1960, the company built plants in Kingstree and Dillon which operated production lines until 1974. That year all production was moved to the Florence plant, where it remains today. The plants in Dillon and Kingstree were used as warehouse locations, together with a warehouse in Georgetown.

In 1979 the company bought the Dr. Pepper-Mountain Dew local franchise and added these two products to the Pepsi, Diet Pepsi, Teem, Patio Orange, and Nugrape lines it was producing. Shortly thereafter, Sunkist was added. The addition of products and sales growth necessitated the addition of a new production line. In 1987 the company purchased the local franchise for Canada Dry products and the Seven-Up franchise in 1989. The most recent addition has been the Lipton Tea and OceanSpray products in 1993.

In an effort to bring additional variety to the business in 1992, the company began Pee Dee Food Service, a full-line, vending machine food products company. Pee Dee Food Service has experienced tremendous growth and in 1995 purchased Southeast Vending, another local full-line vendor. Today Pee Dee Food Service serves customers in six counties in the Pee Dee area.

Pepsi Cola Bottling Company's present location on David McLeod Boulevard in Florence

The company moved to its present-day location at 2300 David McLeod Boulevard in 1974. Frank, Fred, and George Avent, sons of the founder, as well as Robert Medlin, a son-in-law, now take active roles in the management of the business and continue his spirit of enterprise and service in the Florence community.

Pee Dee Electric Cooperative, Inc.

The history of Pee Dee Electric Cooperative, Inc. is an important part of the modernization of the Pee Dee region of South Carolina. Without the Co-op, many people in the rural areas would be without the benefits of electricity—benefits such as lights, hot water heaters, washing machines, refrigerators, and the many other appliances that are taken for granted.

Before Pee Dee Electric Cooperative was founded in December of 1939, the daily activities of a rural woman consisted of carrying water to be boiled, hand washing loads of dirty laundry, rinsing the laundry in wash tubs filled with more boiling water, and hanging the loads of laundry to dry. She did this while having to cook on a wood cookstove, care for the children, and see to other everyday chores. If it rained, she was in trouble. And that was just Monday. On Tuesday she ironed clothes with a seven-pound stove-heated iron that had to be held with a cloth, so as to not burn her hand.

Pee Dee Electric began with a core group of 345 customers and 147 pole miles of electric power lines. Today, the Co-op serves over 23,000 meters and maintains 3,283 pole miles of line, serving residential, commercial, and industrial customers throughout the Pee Dee.

When the lights came on in the rural areas of the Pee Dee, it changed things forever. Children no longer had to study by a kerosene lamp; radios brought entertainment and news into the home; and everyone could take a bath at night! Pee Dee Electric Cooperative means more to people than just electric power at reasonable rates. The Cooperative promotes economic development which leads to good paying jobs. It is a source of digital satellite system home entertainment for all; and as an economic force in the area, the Cooperative is dedicated to providing its member/owners a voice locally, statewide, and at the national level.

Pee Dee Electric is a cooperative nonprofit membership corporation organized under the laws of the State of South Carolina, pursuant to the Rural Electric Cooperative Act. Each person receiving power from Pee Dee Electric Cooperative is a member/owner and has a vote in choosing the Board of Trustees which governs operation of the Co-op.

Because of its nonprofit status, Pee Dee Electric returns all excess revenues, over and above the cost of doing business, to the member/owners in the form of capital credit checks each year. As consumers, the member/owners spend and invest these capital credit refunds in the Pee Dee region, improving the quality of life and the prosperity of area businesses. Between 1954 and 1996, Pee Dee Electric Cooperative returned nearly $17 million dollars to its member/owners for circulation in the local economy and

Robert W. Williams Jr., Pee Dee Electric's executive vice president and general manager, addresses the member/owners at the 56th Annual Meeting. Those seated include *from the right:* South Carolina Governor David Beasley, former Congressman and Executive Vice President and General Manager of NRECA Glenn English, the Honorable John Spratt, U.S. Congressman, and T. B. Cunningham, secretary-treasurer of Pee Dee Electric Cooperative.

marketplace. Additionally, Pee Dee Electric Cooperative pays property and sales taxes, franchise fees, and other forms of taxes, excluding income tax, on an annual basis. In 1995, the local and state taxes and fees paid out totaled $1,145,654.

Member/owners at registration for the 56th Annual Meeting of Pee Dee Electric Cooperative, Inc.

As an incentive to industries looking to the Pee Dee region for possible expansion, the Cooperative maintains the Pee Dee Regional Conference Center at the Florence Regional Airport. The Center, by virtue of its location on the airport, provides the accommodations of comfort and convenience, as well as the seclusion preferred by visiting CEOs and their representatives. The facility's boardroom is equipped with the latest communications and audiovisual capabilities, along with a full-service kitchen. Herein, anonymity can be maintained, as principals discuss and negotiate economic growth and new investment in plants and facilities for the Pee Dee.

Pee Dee Electricom, Inc., a wholly owned subsidiary of Pee Dee Electric Cooperative, is an authorized RCA dealer. Through this subsidiary, Pee Dee Electric Cooperative first delivered television entertainment into homes on the farm, when and where the cable industry would not make the investment to bring service to rural areas. Today, Pee Dee Electricom serves the Pee Dee with the latest technology in high-powered digital satellite systems and programming. Through the sale of RCA audio and visual equipment, digital satellite systems which bring CD quality video and audio through an 18-inch dish, and as the agent for DIRECTV programming throughout the seven-county area, Pee Dee Electric Cooperative, through its subsidiary, Pee Dee Electricom, serves to provide a better quality of life in yet another way.

Throughout its history, Pee Dee Electric Cooperative has always sought to better serve its member/owners. In 1965 Pee Dee Electric merged with Marion Electric Cooperative, creating a much larger and stronger electric utility, one better suited to influence power suppliers and obtain the lowest possible rates for electricity. Pee Dee Electric's customers enjoy rates lower than those of any competing electric utility. Further, continuous training of employees and implementation of state-of-the-art technology assures Pee Dee Electric's position of leadership in the Pee Dee community.

The employees of the Co-op represent a cross section of Pee Dee residents. They maintain a sense of service to the member/owners and a steadfast commitment to the community. Many volunteer their time and resources to local churches and charitable organizations and some serve on boards and commissions throughout the Pee Dee.

The Cooperative's Board of Trustees is made up of community leaders representing the Cooperatives's area. These individuals have the knowledge and dedication to serve the member/owners in a competent and forward-thinking manner. Their goal is to maintain Pee Dee Electric Cooperative's position and status as the best utility in South Carolina.

Mr. Robert W. Williams Jr., the executive vice president and general manager of Pee Dee Electric Cooperative, keeps the Cooperative on the cutting edge of technology and economic development. As recipient of the Order of the Palmetto, the state's highest honor, he is recognized as an expert in rural electrification and a major contributor to the achievement of economic growth in the Pee Dee region. He is known worldwide for his service to the United States State Department and for his work in foreign lands, to help other governments build rural electric programs and systems.

Pee Dee Electric was formed in 1939 because investor-owned utilities would not invest money to build lines to sparsely populated rural areas. The investor-owned utilities considered the costs of construction to be too great for the small return they would receive. Then, as now, Pee Dee Electric is dedicated to providing dependable electric service at a reasonable price. This will continue to be the single most deciding factor in the continued growth of Pee Dee Electric Cooperative, Inc., serving commercial, residential, and industrial member/owners throughout the Pee Dee.

Young Pecan Company

In 1993 Young Pecan Company had become the largest pecan sheller in this industry, having started as the smallest in 1945. In the past, it had employed up to 400 people in the Florence plant and up to 1,000 at its three plants. Through an effort to reduce costs and be more competitive, these numbers have been substantially reduced by modern technology, including laser, infrared, electronic sorting, and other equipment. The company now has the trained personnel, management, and facilities to position it for a very competitive future of worldwide operations with a capacity of shelling 80 million pounds of in-shell pecans annually.

Part of a complicated process of cracking and shelling, a high speed infrared process color sorts pecan meats one particle at a time. Darker colored kernels are separated from lighter colored kernels.

Thomas Benton Young Sr. (1882-1960) was the founder of the predecessors of Young Pecan Company. He graduated from Clemson A&M College in 1903 with a major in agriculture, and returned to his home, Florence, to begin his career in South Carolina agriculture. In 1904 he introduced hot red cayenne peppers as a new crop in the Florence area, which then became a major money crop in Florence and Darlington Counties. This crop was marketed through the Carolina Pepper Association until 1969. He introduced additional crops in the Pee Dee region and formed the Sweet Potato Association and the South Carolina Peach Association. These crops and others were marketed under the name of Carolina's Co-operatives Consolidated, which Young managed. In addition, he engaged in the marketing of several other crops grown in the Pee Dee region, including green beans, peas, squash, honeydew melons, and dewberries, along with pecans.

At that time, pecans were purchased throughout the Carolinas and marketed in-shell to supermarket chains, including Atlantic and Pacific Tea Company (A&P) and others. Any excess were marketed to shellers. Young started other agricultural enterprises, including a farm machinery business, Planters Produce and Storage Company, and the distribution of insecticides, chemicals, and fertilizer. The names of these enterprises were changed in 1949 to Planters Equipment and Supply Company.

In 1932 he retired due to a heart attack, although he continued to exercise the leadership of his business through a manager, Paul H. Gee. In 1942 he formed T. B. Young and Company to handle the produce and pecan side of the business. By then all of the cooperatives had ceased to exist or moved away, leaving the pecan business as the only agricultural survivor.

His son, J. Givens Young, returned from military service in World War II in 1945 and started a pecan shelling plant in Florence, specializing in this particular crop as part of his father's business. The Carolina pecans are of good quality and particularly well-suited for shelling. Givens Young quickly learned the mechanical shelling process and began to improve, streamline, and modernize it. Marketing of the shelled pecans was initiated through local food brokers in major cities and also to old friends such as the A&P Tea Company.

Business grew through emphasis on quality, service, competitive prices, and many hours of hard work. The plant was enlarged, and capacity increased over the years. In 1956 Givens Young became the sole owner of the pecan business. That year the shelling plant was moved to a larger site next door,

Young Pecan Company Shelling Plant and Headquarters at Florence, South Carolina

The final step in the process, visual inspection of pecan meats insures that every kernel is perfect prior to shipment.

and additional plant space was built onto the existing warehouse. In 1959 the plant was modernized, and more space was added to the warehouse.

In 1963 the company's first freezer for storage of in-shell and shelled pecans was built. The name of the business was changed to Young Pecan Shelling Company, Inc., and several subsidiary corporations were formed, including Young Pecan Sales Corporation. About that time, Givens Young bought Calhoun Pecan Company of St. Matthews, South Carolina, and Haygood Pecan Company of Lexington, South Carolina, and added their Fund Raising and Mail Order Gift Pack sales outlets. In 1968 substantial plant space was added. In 1973 another four-million-pound capacity freezer was added, and in 1977 another building was added for receiving, processing, and storage of in-shell pecans. Another freezer was added in 1981, making a total of 12 million pounds of freezer storage on site.

During these years, the capacity of the plant was increased, upgraded, and modernization was continued. Volume and sales continued to increase. Young Pecan became a major supplier, and in some cases the sole source, to blue-chip national and international food manufacturing companies who use pecans to enhance their products. This list reads like a "who's who" in the baking, ice cream, confectionery, cereal, and other food industries.

In 1985 the South Carolina Chamber of Commerce commissioned the accounting firm of Arthur Andersen to determine the largest 100 independently owned South Carolina-based businesses. During the ensuing years, Young Pecan has continuously been one of the "South Carolina 100," ranked from number 99 to the current number 26, and the only Florence business ranked in this group.

In 1985 James W. Swink Jr. came on board and began to learn all facets of the business. His specialty was marketing, and sales increased at a fast rate. Pecan production was expanding rapidly in Mexico, West Texas, and New Mexico. In 1987 a new plant was built by the company in Mexico across the border from El Paso, Texas, to take advantage of western production. Nut Tree Pecan Company of Albany, Georgia, was acquired in 1988, which gave Young a base in the major pecan producing area of Georgia. Also Goodbee Pecan Plantations was acquired, a major Mail Order Gift Pack sales organization. With three state-of-the-art plants, all strategically located, Young began marketing overseas, and exports grew rapidly.

In 1992 Young made its most significant move by merging its pecan operation with the pecan operation of Gold Kist, Inc., of Atlanta, Georgia, a very large diversified agribusiness. Young maintained its management plus 75 percent ownership, and Gold Kist added substantial financial strength and marketing input. James Swink became president and CEO, while Givens Young, after 50 years, became chairman of the Partnership Committee and consultant.

In 1995 Young Pecan began its diversification into the other tree nuts by creating a partnership with a Central American macadamia operation. This expansion into macadamia nuts parallels Young's efforts to provide high quality luxury nuts to all facets of the world nut industry. Young Pecan continues its global marketing efforts and recently opened a direct-marketing office for western Europe in Brussels.

Young Pecan's predecessors started in Florence 90 years ago and started shelling pecans 50 years ago. Its products and services have expanded from a national market to an international market where its name is well known for pecans and other nuts. Young and Swink attribute much of the credit for the company's growth to their many fine and faithful employees who have worked long and hard over the years. The main operation is here, and it is proud to continue to be headquartered in Florence, South Carolina.

J. Givens Young with boxes of Young's shelled pecans ready for shipment

The Florence Army Air Base was created just after the United States entered World War II. The city purchased 200 acres at the airfield for a camp to house 2,700 members of the Army Air Force.

International Knife & Saw

International Knife & Saw, (IKS) Florence Operation, is part of a company which is the world's leading source of industrial machine knives and saws. With an extensive network of specialized divisions that are convenient to all parts of the world, IKS offers diversified products and comprehensive services to a wide variety of industries. The company's mission is to continually improve its products and services to meet customers' needs, allowing it to prosper as a business, create new jobs, and to provide customers with a product they will want to continue buying in the future.

IKS goes back over 150 years with skilled toolmakers in Remscheid, Germany. Its history in Florence began in 1944, when J. S. Hanna (1894-1964) founded Florence Saw Works. His son, J. L. Hanna, took over in the 1960s and began the rapid expansion and relocation to its present facility on North Cashua Road, where the company was known as "HANNACO." This original facility consisted of an office and factory space of 7,200 square feet. Beginning in 1967, IKS has expanded to its present 110,000-square-foot facility. This growth was made possible over the years due to customer satisfaction and the dedicated, loyal employees of IKS. Presently, IKS has, in Florence, approximately 220 employees in sales, service, general administrative, and production toolmaking.

Each IKS operation not only produces new replacement cutting tools, but it also offers to its customers the opportunity to recondition or sharpen the tools many times thereafter. This additional service allows IKS to keep in close touch with its customer base. Service, time and again after the sale, is a trademark of IKS.

To further ensure customer satisfaction in the finest possible products, IKS cutting tools incorporate the latest technological advances and are manufactured to close tolerance quality control standards. The company's plant in Florence is equipped with the latest CNC laser technology. In addition to its state-of-the-art manufacturing process, the skilled craftsmen at IKS still incorporate old-world toolmaking technology such as hammering (smithing), which insures proper tensioning and flatness of cutting tools. The company's specialized heat treating process insures that IKS knives and saws have the best possible wear resistance and toughness. The end result is performance–the company matches the proper knife or saw to its customers' applications.

The Florence operation of IKS continues its growth by mastering opportunities to produce tools that help its customers increase their production and quality. Due to this unmatched quality and its goal of being the low-cost producer in the industry, IKS will continue to introduce new projects every year to grow its operation.

Although its customer base is worldwide, IKS has found the community of Florence and the Pee Dee area as a whole to be very conducive to its success as an organization. Combined, these attributes make the IKS Florence, South Carolina, operation the largest of the company's facilities worldwide.

Thanks to its employees, the future is bright, and IKS looks for continued growth in the tools it produces and the industries it serves.

IKS cutting tools

Vulcraft

Vulcraft is an industry which was developed locally, prospered, and became an integral part of Nucor Corporation, a corporation engaged in the manufacture of steel products for the domestic and international market.

Vulcraft was incorporated on June 12, 1946. The president and chief stockholder was Sanborn Chase Jr. (1919-61). Chase, a native Florentine and a grandson of Jerome P. Chase Sr., was educated in the public schools of Florence. He received a bachelor of science degree from Auburn University. During World War II, Chase was employed as a physicist by the United States Navy, where he worked in the Charlestown Navy Yard, Boston, Massachusetts. Vulcraft was founded by him when he returned to Florence at the end of World War II. Initially, Vulcraft operated as a machine shop, manufacturing specialty items. It also engaged in various sidelines, such as the sale of chain-link fences and Quonset™ huts.

In 1957 Vulcraft began the fabrication of steel joists, trusses, and beams, and it became the principal supplier of fabricated steel in the Southeast. Chase died in July, 1961, and, following his death, the company was managed for a year by his widow, the former Madge Humphrey.

In 1962 Vulcraft was purchased by Nuclear Corporation of America (Nucor) and became the Vulcraft Division of that corporation. The first general manager which Nucor sent to Florence was Francis Kenneth Iverson. Iverson, a native of Downers Grove, Illinois, remained in Florence from 1962 to 1963. Now chairman of Nucor, he is recognized as one of the outstanding corporate executives in this country. Iverson has been the subject of an extensive profile in the *New Yorker* magazine in 1991; *Business Week* in 1988, 1990, and 1994; and *Forbes* magazine in 1993. He lives in Charlotte, North Carolina, where Nucor's corporate offices are located.

Steel joists awaiting delivery to building projects on the East Coast from Maine to Florida

There are approximately 400 persons employed in the Florence plant. Vulcraft is the nation's largest producer of steel joists and joist girders, which are produced and marketed through six Vulcraft facilities. It also produces steel deck for building construction. This is a major area of operations for Nucor Corporation. Joists and joist girders are used extensively as part of the support systems in manufacturing buildings, retail stores, shopping centers, warehouses, schools, churches, hospitals, and, to a lesser extent, in multistory buildings, apartments, and single-family dwellings. There are five other facilities of Vulcraft Divisions located in Nebraska, Alabama, Texas, Indiana, and Utah.

Steel joists and joist girders sales are obtained by competitive bidding. Vulcraft quotes on an estimated 80 percent to 90 percent of the domestic buildings using steel joists and

Vulcraft plant in 1996

joist girders as part of the support systems. In 1994 Vulcraft supplied more than an estimated 40 percent of the total domestic sales of these products.

Steel deck is used extensively in floors and roofs. Steel deck is specified in about 90 percent of buildings using steel joists and joist girders. Vulcraft steel deck sales increased to 207,000 tons in 1994 from 170,000 tons in 1993.

The increased level of construction since 1994 has favorably impacted the volume of nonresidential buildings supplied by Vulcraft. Vulcraft has the available capacity to increase its production of steel joists, joist girders, and steel deck by more than 25 percent. Almost all of the production employees of Vulcraft work with a group incentive system, which provides increased compensation each week for increased production. A similar incentive plan was instituted by Sanborn Chase in the 1950s.

In the neighboring county of Darlington, Nucor has two major plants in the Nucor Steel Division and the Nucor Cold Finish Division. The Nucor Steel Division is engaged in the

Steel deck materials loaded on trucks scheduled for delivery

manufacture of steel which is produced as bars, angles, light structural, sheet, and special steel products. In addition to selling steel on the open market, these steel mills assure an economical supply of steel for the Vulcraft, Nucor Cold Finish, Nucor Grinder Balls, Nucor Fastener, and Nucor Building Systems operations.

All six Nucor Steel mills are among the most modern and efficient mills in the United States. Steel scrap is melted in electric arc furnaces and poured into continuous casting systems. Highly sophisticated rolling mills convert the billets and slabs into angles, rounds, channels, flats, sheet, and other products. The operations in the rolling mills are highly automated and require fewer operating employees than older mills.

The Darlington plant also is a part of Nucor Cold Finish Divisions. Cold finished steel products are used extensively for shafting and machined precision parts. Nucor Cold Finish produces rounds, hexagons, flats, and squares in carbon and alloy steels.

Darlington and the other two facilities are among the most modern in the world and use inline electronic testing to insure outstanding quality. Nucor Cold Finish obtains most of its steel from nearby Nucor Steel mills. This factor, along with its efficient newer facilities, results in highly competitive pricing.

On the international side of the corporation's activity is the Nucor-Yamato Steel Company. In 1988 Nucor and Yamato Kogo, one of Japan's major producers of wide-flange beams, completed construction and started operation of a new steel mill to produce wide-flange beams, pilings, and heavy structural steel products near

Vulcraft plant in the 1950s

Blytheville, Arkansas. This steel mill, in which Nucor has a 51 percent interest, now has an annual capacity of 1.8 million tons. In 1994 Nucor-Yamato Steel shipped over 1.6 million tons of finished and semifinished steel products.

Nucor plans to build a new thin-slab steel mill in Berkley County, South Carolina. This new mill will cost approximately $500 million and will have an annual capacity close to 1.8 million tons. Full operations are expected to begin early in 1997. This will bring Nucor's total steel-making capacity close to 10 million tons per year.

Nucor has a strong sense of loyalty and responsibility to its employees. It has not closed a single facility and has maintained the stability of its workforce for many years. The productivity of employees is high and employee relations are good. In 1994 Nucor generated $502,000 of sales per employee.

Florence Urological Association

Florence Urological Association offers a medical specialty to the Pee Dee region which grew out of the expansion of medical services in Florence during the 1920s. Its growth demonstrated the advantage of having medical specialists who render services to all of the hospitals in Florence and to hospitals in the Pee Dee region.

The Urological Association had its beginning when Dr. Frank H. McLeod brought Dr. Orin T. Finklea (1895-1959) to practice in the McLeod Infirmary. Although he did not have that particular specialty at the time he came to Florence, Dr. Finklea eventually became a specialist in urology.

Dr. Finklea was born in Hyman, South Carolina, attended Furman University, and the Medical College of South Carolina where he received an M.D. degree. He saw brief service in the United States Navy Medical Corps in World War I, and came to Florence in 1919. He went to the University of Pennsylvania for training in radiology and for special training in urology at Johns Hopkins. On his return, he then created a department of urology at the Florence Infirmary.

Dr. Finklea was active in many civic organizations. He served as chairman of the Florence City School Board for eight years and was elected president of the South Carolina School Board Association. A member of the First Baptist Church in Florence, he served on the board of deacons and as chairman of the finance committee.

The growth of his practice caused Dr. Finklea to bring in Dr. Eugene Daniel Guyton Sr. as a partner. Dr. Guyton was born in Charleston, South Carolina, but he moved to Marion at an early age. A 1938 graduate of Clemson University, and the Medical College of South Carolina in 1942, he came to Florence to do a three-year residency and was assigned to work with Dr. Finklea. World War II interrupted his stay and he spent three years in the United States Navy attaining the rank of lieutenant.

In 1946 he resumed his professional relationship with Dr. Finklea as a three-year apprenticeship in urology. They eventually formed a partnership, which was located in the Florence Trust Building. During the early days of the partnership, the partners practiced exclusively in the McLeod Infirmary. Dr. Guyton, however, began to respond to requests for his services at both Saunders Memorial and Bruce Hospitals. This set a pattern which other specialists would follow and enhanced the health care available at all three hospitals.

The death of Dr. Finklea in 1959 created the immediate need of Dr. Guyton to secure another qualified urologist. Dr. E. W. "Casey" Taylor came to Florence and entered into the partnership. Dr. Taylor was born and raised in eastern North Carolina. He was graduated from Oakridge Military Academy and Wake Forest College and received his medical degree from Bowman Gray School of Medicine in 1953. He did an internship in surgery at Duke University (1953-54); one year residency in urology at Roper Hospital (1954-55); served in the United States Army Medical Corps (1955-57), attaining the rank of captain; second and third year urological residency at the Medical University of South Carolina (1957-59); and came to Florence in July, 1959.

Dr. Taylor is certified by the American Board of Urology and served as president of the South Carolina Urological Association (1979). He is married to the former Peggy Ann Lee, and they have two children and two grandchildren.

Benjamin K. Ward Jr. joined the practice in 1974. Born in Goldsboro, North Carolina, he attended the undergraduate and Medical School at the University of North Carolina at Chapel Hill, finishing in 1967. He is married to Anne Starr Minton from Greensboro, North Carolina, and they have two children. After two years of duty on a Navy destroyer, Dr. Ward did a urology residency at the University of Alabama Medical School, finishing in

1974. His wife, a violinist, required that they locate in a city with a symphony orchestra, and Florence fulfilled that requirement.

He is the past chief of staff of Florence General Hospital, past president of the Florence Rotary Club, past president and executive board member of Pee Dee Area Big Brothers, and is heavily involved in church and mission work.

Dr. Eugene Daniel Guyton Jr. joined the practice in 1977. Guyton was born in Florence, South Carolina, in 1944. He was educated in Florence public schools, graduated from Davidson College in 1966, and from the Medical University of South Carolina in 1970. Dr. Guyton did internship and residency in UAB Hospitals and Clinics. He served in the United States Army Medical Corps (1972-74). Dr. Guyton is an Episcopalian and has served as a vestryman at All Saints Episcopal Church. He also serves on the board of Habitat for Humanity and of Florence Arts Council. He is married to the former Susan Chasteen of Florence, and they have two children.

Dr. Stuart Alan Greenberg joined the practice in July, 1980. He was born in 1949 in Florence. His father, Dr. Steven A. Greenberg, was a physician in Florence. Dr. Greenberg was educated in the Florence public schools and the Asheville School in North Carolina, attended Duke University and was graduated from the University of South Carolina with a B.S. degree in 1971, received his medical degree from the Medical University of South Carolina in 1975, did a general surgery residency with the Louisiana State University Medical Center at Charity Hospital, New Orleans, and a residency in urology at the University of Alabama Hospital Systems in Birmingham.

He has served as chief of staff of Florence General Hospital, and his civic activities include service on the Florence Airport Commission, the City of Florence Zoning and Variance Commission, board membership at All Saints Episcopal Day School, and membership on the board of directors of Francis Marion University Foundation. Dr. Greenberg is married to the former Rebecca Bernos of New Orleans, Louisana, and they have two children. He and his family attend Temple Beth Israel, where he has served as president of the Temple affiliates.

Dr. James Kevin O'Kelly joined the practice in 1993. Dr. O'Kelly was born in Toronto, Canada, in 1958. He received his B.S. degree from the University of South Carolina in 1980 and an M.D. degree from St. George's University in 1986. Dr. O'Kelly did his internship at Methodist Hospital, New York, and a residency at both Methodist Hospital and the University of South Florida Medical College. He is chief of surgery at Carolinas Hospital System and sits on the advisory board of First National South Bank.

Dr. O'Kelly married the former Carol Worthington-Metz of Columbia, South Carolina, in 1984. They have a son and a daughter.

***Seated, left to right:* Dr. Eugene Daniel Guyton Jr., Dr. Benjamin K. Ward Jr. *Standing, left to right:* Dr. E. W. "Casey" Taylor, Dr. James Kevin O'Kelly, Dr. Stuart Alan Greenberg**

The Atlantic Broadcasting Company

WJMX, a radio station that has become a communications leader in the Pee Dee region, went on the air in 1947. Paul H. Benson Jr. (1915-90) was the organizer, chief stockholder, and president of the Atlantic Broadcasting Company, which owned WJMX. Benson started the first motor racing network broadcast from the Darlington Raceway, which later became the Motor Racing Network carrying NASCAR. The original board and MIC used by Benson are now part of the collection of the South Carolina State Museum. In addition, Benson was given a license for WSTN, an FM station known as a Beautiful Music Station.

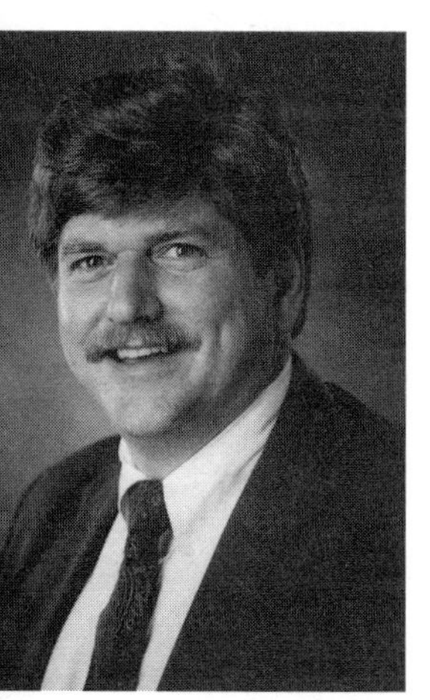

Harold T. Miller, Jr. - president and chief executive officer of The Atlantic Broadcasting Company

In 1985 the Atlantic Broadcasting Company was purchased by present owners Fred Avent, Frank Avent, George Avent, John A. "Jack" Jeffords, and Harold T. Miller. The purchase included both WJMX and WSTN, whose call letters were changed to WJMX-FM, and it became a rock station. The corporate offices are located in Florence and it employs approximately 50 people.

The holdings of the company now include six separate stations.

WJMX-FM 103X, the direct successor of the original station, is a 50,000-watt adult contemporary station that is targeted to reach well-educated, upscale adults in the 18-49 age group, with significant strength in both the older and younger age groups. It carries the number one morning show in the Southeast, the *John Boy and Billy Big Show,* delivered by satellite from WRFX in Charlotte, North Carolina.

WJMX-AM NEWSTALK 970 provides strong local news and discussions of community issues, as well as nationally syndicated programming such as Rush Limbaugh, Alan Colmes, and Bruce Williams. It is the only newstalk radio in the Pee Dee region, and *Kinard 'n Koffee* is the only local radio program featuring a heavy emphasis on local news events and interviews with community leaders. It also carries the University of South Carolina football and basketball games.

WSQN-FM SUNNY 102.9 is a soft, adult contemporary station. It is a music intensive station with a light commercial load. It is designed to attract the same listeners as Newstalk, since it has long periods of listening, even during business hours. The programs are rebroadcast on the company's repeater station 95.3-FM.

WGTR-FM GATOR 107.9 is a 50,000-watt station targeted to reach the 25-54 age group. The station offers broad coverage from the Charleston County line to the North Carolina border. It is the company's hot country station in Myrtle Beach, which features the most popular country music hits available.

WDAR-FM GATOR 105.5 is the company's newest hot country station located in Darlington, South Carolina. It has been upgraded to a 25,000-watt station and has the same format as WGTR-FM in Myrtle Beach.

WWSK-FM 107.1–THE SHARK, in Myrtle Beach, is the company's newest 50,000-watt station with an adult contemporary format targeting well-educated adults, both residents and tourists. Stations are planned for Ocean Isle, North Carolina, to begin broadcasting in 1996 and Kingstree, South Carolina, in 1997.

Atlantic Broadcasting Company is the emergency broadcast station for the Pee Dee region. It renders other essential and invaluable community service by providing a forum for discussion of local issues, and promoting civic projects such as McLeod Children's Hospital, the March of Dimes, community blood drives, and many others throughout the Pee Dee.

The signals of Atlantic Broadcasting Company stations in eastern South and North Carolina

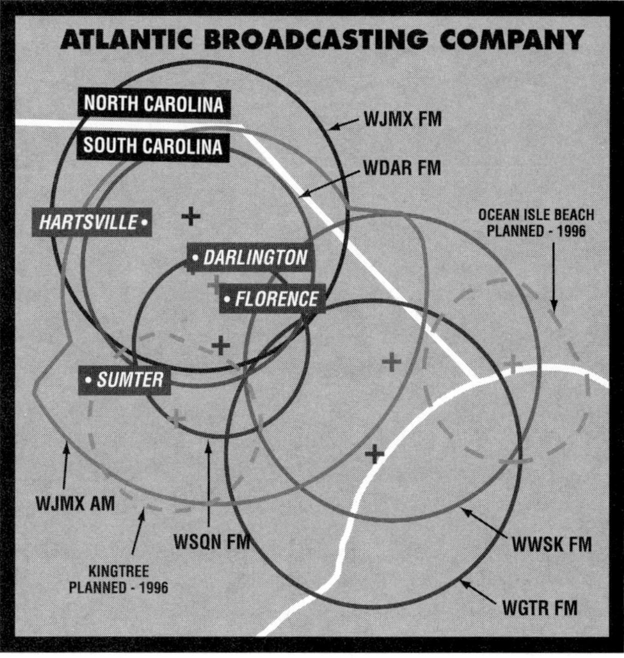

Darlington Raceway

Darlington Raceway, located some 12 miles from the city of Florence in Darlington County, is NASCAR'S original superspeedway. Its presence is tangible evidence of the triumph of the motor car not only as a means of transportation but as a symbol which inspires mass enthusiasm for advanced mechanical engineering, speed, and design.

An aerial view of Darlington Raceway, NASCAR's original superspeedway

The city of Florence and the Pee Dee region of South Carolina have greatly benefitted from the tourism generated by NASCAR races at the Darlington Raceway. Two Florence County residents have played a significant part in the Raceway's development and history–the late Walter D. "Red" Tyler (1921-94) and three-time NASCAR Winston Cup Champion Cale Yarborough, who won a record five Mountain Dew Southern 500s.

When Darlington resident Harold Brasington (1909-96) constructed NASCAR's original superspeedway in 1950, no one, not even Harold, knew the magnitude of its role in the history and evolution of NASCAR.

While through the years Raceway officials have tinkered with the cantankerous facility, adding numerous ultramodern improvements for the fans and competitors alike, the track, with its almost human disposition, is still the same as always. It's mean, ornery, and very much capable of making grown men cry. It truly is "Too Tough to Tame."

There have been a select few to triumph at Darlington–legendary greats like Richard Petty, David Pearson, Fireball Roberts, Cale Yarborough, Bobby Allison, Buck Baker, and Fred Lorenzen. Today, it's names like Darrell Waltrip, Bill Elliott, and seven-time NASCAR Winston Cup Series Champion, Dale Earnhardt, who needs to beat Darlington just once more to tie Pearson's all-time Darlington win record of 10 triumphs. They all have won, but no one has ever finessed Darlington.

Brasington broke ground on December 13, 1949. "Where the track sits now was farmland that belonged to Mr. Sherman Ramsey," Brasington once related. "He was hesitant at first, but then agreed to let me have the property. So we started right there, on a handshake. I knew what I wanted. I knew the size I wanted. I knew we needed grandstands, restrooms, and concession stands. I got my equipment up and started plowing and moving dirt."

Harold's vision of NASCAR's first paved superspeedway was that of a true oval, but a minnow pond changed those plans. "Mr. Ramsey had a minnow pond just outside turn two, and he didn't want it disturbed," added Brasington, "so we had to draw the track in, giving it its unique, egg-shaped layout."

With the help of NASCAR founder Bill France Sr., who agreed to sanction the race, a field of 75 showed up for the inaugural event on the new 1.25-mile high-banked track. They expected a mere 10,000 spectators; over 25,000 showed up. Brasington's dream had become a reality.

In 1952 Bob Colvin replaced Brasington as president. An innovator and one of the sport's best-known promoters, Colvin started making changes quickly. In 1953 turns one and two were lengthened and banked steeper (23 degrees), making the distance around the track 1.375 miles.

The year 1957 saw another event added to Darlington's schedule. NASCAR's convertible division made its debut, creating two major weekends for South Carolina's biggest little city.

Harold Brasington *(right)* confers with Louis Piana on the construction plans for Darlington Raceway in 1949.

Pit stops are poetry in motion at Darlington. Here, Ricky Rudd gets quick service during the 1995 TranSouth Financial 400.

That event today is known as the TranSouth Financial 400.

In 1968 the flat third and fourth turns were reworked, and banked to 25 degrees. The project was headed by track President Barney Wallace, who took over the controls of the track in 1967. The track was remeasured to its present measurement of 1.366 miles in 1970.

In 1982 International Speedway Corporation purchased the track, and a year later, Tyler became president. It was during his tenure that the construction of numerous buildings, including new restrooms, and rebuilding the concrete outer and pit walls were completed.

Today, Darlington hosts two major NASCAR racing weekends–the TranSouth race in the spring, and the Mountain Dew Southern 500 each Labor Day weekend.

There's "old" and "new" at Darlington as it prepares for the future. The "old" is tradition, history, and heritage that will always linger when one breathes the words "Darlington Raceway."

The "new" is vaulting itself into the twenty-first century, and in a hurry. The man at the controls is a South Carolina native, who returned to his roots in January of 1993 to become president of the raceway.

Jim Hunter, from North Charleston, was Darlington Raceway's public relations director in the mid-1960s, and became one of the guiding forces in helping NASCAR become the country's largest spectator sport. Prior to coming "home," he was NASCAR's vice president of administration and marketing at corporate headquarters in Daytona Beach, Florida, for 11 years.

Under his guidance, Darlington Raceway has shifted into high gear. Massive improvements have taken place at the raceway. The new ultramodern, state-of-the-art "Tyler Tower" was constructed and now sits high atop the backstretch, complete with ultramodern restrooms, food courts, and souvenir stands.

Other restroom facilities around the track have been reworked, numerous buildings have been constructed, and now every ticket purchaser has a chairback seat. Colorful, blooming flowers are planted everywhere, and palmettos (the state tree of South Carolina) stand tall. Lush green grass covers the infield and the outskirts of the track. It's become the "Augusta National" of stock car racing.

The facility has also become a full-fledged community, corporate citizen, hosting numerous charitable events, including "Santa's Workshop," each December, in which the NASCAR garage is transformed into a Christmas Winter Wonderland which attracts more than 5,000 people.

Darlington's community service helps raise money for various local charities such as the Children's Hospital at McLeod Regional Medical Center in Florence and the Pee Dee Education Foundation.

Numerous high school and college programs have been instituted, along with a scholarship in the name of Harold Brasington, which goes to a deserving high school senior in the Palmetto State.

The Raceway caters to South Carolina businesses, developing programs for entrepreneurial startup companies so they will be a part of the Raceway's continuous growth–a growth which calls for additional seating, corporate suites, and continuing improvements to fulfill its corporate mission statement of being the best facility in motorsports.

1984 NASCAR Winston Cup Series Champion Terry Labonte flashes past the "South Carolina" billboard in turn two.

Aluminum Ladder Company

During 1930, as the economy went from boom to bust, the Aluminum Company of America (ALCOA) asked project engineers to find new uses and markets for its aluminum products. Aluminum was a relatively new material, and supplementary uses were not readily accepted by industry. Additionally, the Depression was deepening, and ALCOA was searching for more sales. The idea to manufacture an aluminum ladder originally came from a solicitation from the Oslo, Norway, Fire Department. The fire department was seeking an alternative to the heavy wood ladders that had been used since fire departments began using ladders. A 50-foot wood extension ladder was extremely heavy and difficult to place in position to fight a fire. One of the ALCOA project engineers, Sam Carbis, submitted the idea to manufacture aluminum ladders to his superior. After discussions by the ALCOA marketing group, ALCOA decided that aluminum ladders did not fit into their corporate strategy. Thus, as the Depression intensified, Sam Carbis resigned from ALCOA and created the Aluminum Ladder Company. With one customer, little money, three employees, and many ideas and dreams, Sam rented a small building in Tarentum, Pennsylvania, to begin manufacturing aluminum ladders.

Sam Carbis survived the Depression by innovative manufacturing and marketing techniques, as well as a great deal of frugality. By the beginning of World War II, Aluminum Ladder Company had 40 employees and had expanded its market to include aluminum industrial stepladders and extension ladders. Sam's idea of a "heavy-duty," "lightweight" ladder that he named the "Alco-Lite" ladder had captured the attention of companies such as E. I. DuPont, Proctor and Gamble, Union Carbide, and others. Sam's ladders could stand the rigorous treatment that heavy industry demanded.

When Sam Carbis became seriously ill in 1944, he turned over the reins to his 24-year-old daughter, Helen Cramer. During the time that women were expected to stay home attending family affairs, Helen was catapulted into the president's position with all the responsibilities related to managing Aluminum Ladder Company. She quickly found that, in wartime, running a company was even more difficult than normal. Aluminum was rationed for the war effort, wages were escalating, employees were hard to find and keep, and many resented a woman managing a business. With determination, a desire to succeed, and a refusal to accept "no" as an answer, Helen finally negotiated a purchase for 15,000 pounds of aluminum to keep production going. Once she received the material, she decided nothing would prevent her success. Customers who refused to accept a female business executive were directed to a draftsman who served as a company spokesman. During a tax audit, the Internal Revenue Service claimed that her $10,000 annual salary was exorbitant for a female and forced her to reduce her pay to equal that of a company clerk.

Near the end of World War II, Helen's husband, Darrell, (1916-68) was wounded and returned home from the European theater. Darrell, also known as "D.D.," rejoined his wife in the company, and together they prospered with Helen controlling the financial areas and Darrell managing the sales and manufacturing areas. By the mid-1950s, the Cramers determined that the company needed to relocate. Travel in the mountainous Pennsylvania was difficult, and in the winter, hazardous. Ladder deliveries and flight plans were constantly changing.

First aluminum ladder made

Additionally, the company had outgrown its two-story manufacturing facilities in Worthington, Pennsylvania.

In searching for new sites, the Cramers discovered Florence, South Carolina. Labor and manufacturing facilities were available, the weather was good, and Florence had an airport. A decision on the best site available was made, and in 1959 Aluminum Ladder Company became the first of a long list of companies to locate in Florence.

Aluminum fire ladder being tested by local fire company

Once relocated to Florence, the company continued to prosper until the death of Darrell Cramer in 1968. Again, Helen Cramer resumed total responsibility for the company. Some problems still remained with a woman in charge, but using the same determination and desire to succeed, Helen continued to manage the company. Fiberglass ladders and mobile steel ladder stands were introduced during this transitional period, and sales grew to $2 million. Her son, Sam Cramer, entered the business in 1969, the third generation to do so. Together, they established Carbis, Incorporated in 1976 to serve as the marketing arm to Aluminum Ladder Company and established Alco-Lite Industries in 1995 to serve the structural and miscellaneous steel markets.

Since that humble beginning in 1930, Aluminum Ladder Company, Carbis, and Alco-Lite Industries have grown approximately 20 percent each year since 1985. Sam Cramer is now president, and Helen serves as chairperson of the board. With 200 total employees, combined sales now surpass $22 million. While not well known in Florence, the companies are recognized throughout the world, with their sales force and 40-employee engineering staff advising all Fortune 500 manufacturing companies on access equipment, fall prevention, bulk loading and unloading, and structural/miscellaneous items. As a result of their reputation in access equipment, the Saudi royal family, after searching world-wide for a solution, commissioned them to design and manufacture a system for changing lights in all of their mosques. Major contacts continue with E. I. DuPont, Union Carbide, Procter and Gamble, BASF, and others. Their office and manufacturing facilities have increased to 116,000 square feet with a 50,000-square-foot expansion planned for the near future.

In asking Helen or Sam Cramer the secret to success, one answer is given. The employees they have here in Florence are the *BEST.* Since relocating to Florence, the company's accomplishments would have been lessened without its people. Of course, if you are asking Helen, you might hear that determination, a desire to succeed, and a refusal to accept "no" as an answer also had some impact. ❧

Sam Carbis on one of the first aluminum ladders

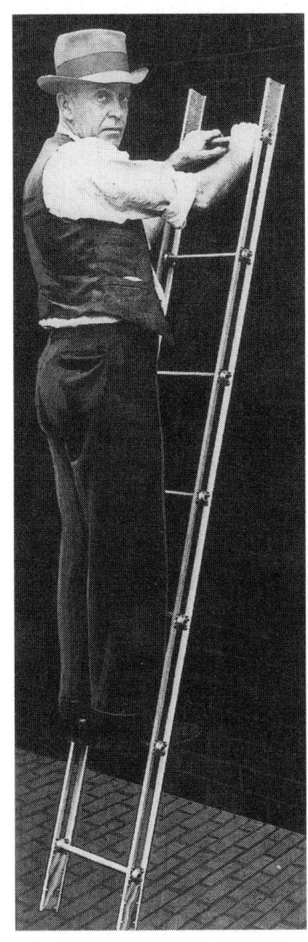

WBTW-TV 13

For over 40 years, WBTW-TV 13, a proud affiliate of CBS, has been a powerful television voice in northeastern South Carolina and southeastern North Carolina. Its current Direct Marketing Area (DMA) includes over 210,000 households and a greater survey market area of more than 370,00 households. Located on the road which took its name, "Television Road," its broadcast studio near Florence is the modern communications hub of the Pee Dee region.

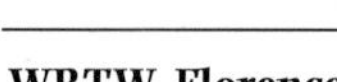

WBTW, Florence

Operations began on October 17, 1954, and the broadcast was on the air only about four or five hours. It was not an auspicious occasion, for it was the day Hurricane Hazel struck the coast of the Carolinas. The station began as a property of Jefferson Pilot Company of Charlotte, North Carolina, and was, in effect, a subsidiary of WBTV-Channel 3, Charlotte. The first managing director was J. William Quinn. The chief engineer was Emil Sellars.

During the early years, as program length increased, numerous local programs were produced. Two of these memorable programs were *Space Ship C-8*, featuring C. James "Capt'n Jim" Player (1923-89), who was succeeded by Ashby Ward, and the *Slim Mim's Show* with Charles "Uncle Ugly" Mims. Clemson's Extension Service was given free broadcast time for a popular program *Southeast Almanac*.

In 1968 ownership was transferred to the Daily Telegraph Printing Company of Bluefield, West Virginia. Joseph B. Foster replaced Quinn as general manager, and Bernard E. "Bernie" Moore, whose service has been a major factor in the station's success, became chief engineer. The station retained, however, its microwave connection with Charlotte. In 1979 the station, under Moore's supervision, constructed a new 2,000-foot tower in Dillon County. It is one of the tallest structures in the United States and is directed toward coverage of the coastal areas, particularly Myrtle Beach and Wilmington. In technical terms, WBTW went to Circularly Polarized (CP) Operation with the tower and a new parallel G-line transmitter. Favorable viewer reaction was received from some located 60 to 90 miles from the transmitter.

The station changed hands again in 1984 when Spartan Radiocasting Corporation bought it. Walter J. Brown (1903-95), the chief executive officer and stockholder of Spartan, took a personal interest in the development and expansion of WBTW. Brown, a native of Spartanburg, South Carolina, had been a confidant and aide of James F. Byrnes.

In 1989 the Florence Market became the Florence/Myrtle Beach Market and

WBTW, Myrtle Beach

experienced remarkable growth of 46 percent. Its audience increased again in 1995 by 20 percent with the addition of Robeson County, North Carolina. Bruce Miller succeeded Foster as general manager. The present general manager is Ms. Lou Kirchen.

Local news excellence has always been one major force behind WBTW's continuing expansion. Channel 13's award-winning Eyewitness News team is one of the highest rated news organizations in the country. More than that, however, is the commitment of the entire staff to public service. Each month, the reporters and anchors visit schools and devote countless hours to charities and community events. With live coverage and appeals, WBTW's Channel 13 has helped many community agencies in their service efforts, including helping to collect clothes and toys for deprived children.

Commitment to advancing technology, to serving the community, and meeting continuing demands for excellence has enabled WBTW to maintain a dominant position in eastern South Carolina and southeastern North Carolina. It has contributed to its receiving the fifth highest in viewing shares of all CBS affiliates nationally.

Griggs Floyd & Grantham

Griggs Floyd & Grantham was incorporated January 16, 1980. Over the last 16 years, the company has been one of the premier real estate companies in the Pee Dee area, specializing in both residential and commercial properties. It has been the company's primary focus to give the best service to the people of Florence and surrounding communities for their real estate needs.

James O. Griggs, president, entered the real estate business in 1972. He has served the residential and commercial real estate business for over 24 years. Griggs is a native of Florence and graduated from the University of South Carolina in 1966 with a Bachelor of Science Degree in Business Administration and from the Law School of the University of South Carolina with a Juris Doctor Degree. He is also a Certified Commercial Investment Member (CCIM). Griggs served as president of the Florence Board of Realtors, president of Florence MLS, and was Realtor of the Year in 1981.

Kaye Floyd-Parris, a native of Danville, Virginia, and a graduate of Radford College, Radford, Virginia, entered the real estate business in June 1980 and became a full partner in 1985. She has been a realtor in the residential business for 16 years and has been a Multi-Million Dollar Producer for many years. Floyd-Parris has obtained the Graduate of the Realtors Institute (GRI) designation and Certified Residential Specialist (CSR) designation. Floyd-Parris has served on numerous boards, and in 1992 received the "Small Business Person of the Year Award," and in 1994 she was the recipient of the "Business Person of the Year Award" from the Florence Chamber of Commerce. She was the first woman to receive this prestigious honor.

David N. Grantham is a native of Florence and is a graduate of the University of South Carolina in Business Administration with a major in Finance and Real Estate. He has been a realtor since 1972 and has obtained the GRI and CRS designations. Grantham served as the president of the Florence Board of Realtors, president of Midday Sertoma, and is a member of the Florence Rotary Club. He was elected Realtor of the Year in 1985 and 1995 by his peers.

Griggs Floyd & Grantham moved into its present location at 515 South Cashua Drive in February, 1980, and became a franchise of Better Homes and Gardens in December, 1980.

***Left to right:* Jim Griggs, David Grantham, and Kaye Floyd-Parris**

Along with listing and selling real estate, Griggs Floyd & Grantham, Inc. has dedicated itself to community work with organizations such as the Greater Florence Chamber of Commerce, Florence County Progress, Florence-Darlington TEC Center, Florence Country Club, Rotary, and many others, including sub-committees for various organizations.

In working with developers, the company was instrumental in the development of various residential subdivisions in and around the Florence area. It not only works for people moving in, out, and around the Florence area, but it also works with many different industries in the relocation of their employees.

The company is a great promoter of the Florence area and its quality of life, and believes it to be a fine place to live, work, and raise a family. Florence attracts people, and Griggs Floyd & Grantham is dedicated to providing them with the very best real estate service possible. Who better to market homes than Better Homes and Gardens, a name that has informed and inspired families for 60 years as they have planned, built, remodeled, furnished, and decorated their homes.

E. I. DuPont de Nemours and Company

In the early 1950s DuPont purchased 954 acres of land 14 miles east of Florence along the Pee Dee River, near Winona. The fact that the DuPont Company was planning to build the first major industrial manufacturing facility in the area heralded a new era in the history of Florence. The product which would be produced was Mylar™ polyester film.

In 1954 Mylar™ was a promising development of DuPont chemical research. Its unusual combination of properties recommended its use in fields where films had never been used before. The first plant to manufacture this new product was located in Circleville, Ohio. Demand for Mylar™ film grew so rapidly that additional manufacturing capacity was needed. On May 7, 1961, the DuPont Florence Plant started up, and post-World War II "industrialization" became a reality in the Pee Dee region.

On January 1, 1800, a French immigrant named Eleuthere Irenee duPont came to the United States to escape the tyrannies of the French Revolution and Napoleon. He set foot on American soil New Year's Day, but it was also the beginning of a new century and the modern era.

Eleuthere Irenee duPont, founder of the DuPont Company

The DuPont Florence Polyester Films manufacturing facility

In 1802, at the urging of Thomas Jefferson, he started a small black gunpowder mill on the banks of Brandywine Creek, in Wilmington, Delaware. For over 100 years the DuPont Company's manufacturing effort was devoted exclusively to explosives products, but a changing economy and demand for new and different products led to diversification. The company became renowned for its research and development with the discovery of such products as "Nylon," the world's first synthetic fiber comparable to nature's fibers, "Neoprene," "Freon," "Lucite," "Teflon," "Lycra," and film products like Mylar™ and Cronar™ manufactured at the DuPont Florence Plant today.

The first plant manager at the Florence Plant was Charles E. Fogg, a veteran of 31 years with the company. Along with 306 full-service employees, his challenge was to safely and efficiently start up the plant and begin earning a return on the $19-million investment in equipment and support facilities in Florence. The determination and commitment of all the employees made this goal a reality. Over the ensuing years, the plant grew to a maximum employment of almost 1,000 full-service employees operating five Mylar™ lines and one Cronar™ line. Cronar™ is also a polyester film product, but with different properties and serving different markets. The Cronar™ manufacturing line was started up in September, 1981.

DuPont Florence has had 10 plant managers over its 35-year history, each bringing different talents and strengths to foster continued growth and improvements in production, quality, and human relations. This has led to continued success for the company and its stockholders and job security for its employees.

The current plant manager is Francine P. Cheeseman, the first woman to hold this position and also the first plant manager to hold the dual role of Global Business Director, bringing the "running of the business" to the heart of Florence.

Polyester films are the end product of a polymerization process using dimethyl terephthalate (DMT) and ethylene glycol as the raw ingredients. These materials are fed into vessels where, in the presence of high temperature and exact pressure control, a chemical reaction occurs forming a polymer. The molten material is pumped to a "casting" machine where a sheet of film is formed. From this point, the film sheet is heated, stretched, cooled, and wound into a large roll of film. The specific processing conditions and roll size are tailored to produce a film which meets the exact specifications of the customer. One variable in Mylar™ and Cronar™ films is their thickness, which varies from 0.00006 inches to 0.014 inches. The product leaving the Florence Plant may be thought of as an "intermediate" product, which is subsequently treated and processed by the customer to make a finished product for a multitude of end-uses, such as food packaging, electric motor insulation, pressure sensitive tapes, protective and decorative laminates, computer tapes, drafting films, wire and cable insulation, roll leaf base, stationary supplies, and satellites.

The end-uses for Cronar™ are not as varied, but are nonetheless important in today's society. Cronar™ is used in the photographic, printing, publishing, and medical X-ray industries.

One manifestation of DuPont Florence's interest in employee welfare is the plant's safety record. From plant manager on down, employees help each other to work safely. Safety training is emphasized for every employee, and frequent safety audits, meetings, and personal reminders are used continually to develop a safe working attitude in every employee.

In recent years, DuPont Florence has been a leader in environmental protection. Millions of dollars have been spent on equipment to regulate and significantly reduce emissions to the environment. Some examples of this equipment include aerobic biological treatment for organic liquids, highly efficient bag houses to purify air discharges, and innovative engineering devices to control excessive noise. In many instances, this equipment not only equals, but exceeds the environmental regulatory requirements. In addition, DuPont Florence recycles waste generated in the polyester film manufacturing process, reducing the need for landfill capacity, a growing concern everywhere.

DuPont Florence believes its duty is not only to make a profit for the stockholders of the company, but also to be a good corporate citizen. This is done by providing a safe work environment for its employees, exercising strong environmental stewardship, by supporting the United Way through significant financial support and employee volunteer time, and by encouraging employee participation in a myriad of community activities involving education, the arts, and charitable activities.

During the 35-year history of the DuPont Florence plant, the business has changed from producing film products for the domestic marketplace. Today, with the shift to a global economy and its accompanying competition from around the world, DuPont has changed and adapted on an unprecedented scale. Just as the DuPont Company diversified early in the 1900s, DuPont Florence is developing new and different strategies to survive by significantly increasing productivity and quality, while reducing costs.

DuPont Florence is the lowest cost producer of polyester film in the world, and its film quality is second to none. With the dedication, hard work, and proven adaptability of its employees, DuPont Florence enters the twenty-first century as founder Irenee duPont did in 1800. As Irenee duPont met many challenges, so the proven capabilities of DuPont Florence's employees bode well for success in continuing to bring "Better Things For Better Living" to the world in the next century.

Sign at the entrance to the DuPont Florence plant

Stone Container Corporation

Florence Mill

Stone Container Corporation expanded into the Florence area in the early 1960s. It is a multinational pulp, paper, and paper packaging company with a product line including containerboard, corrugated containers, kraft paper, paper bags and sacks, market pulp, wood products, and through its investment in Stone-Consolidated Corporation, newsprint and groundwood papers.

Stone is an industry which utilizes the manpower and natural resources of the Pee Dee region. The story of its development bears striking resemblances to the history of the people who originally settled in Florence.

Stone Container Corporation, Florence Mill

Joseph Stone immigrated from Russia in 1888, establishing a residence in Philadelphia and later moving to Chicago. Joseph became a relatively successful salesman for a paper jobber. In 1926 Joseph and two of his sons, Norman and Marvin, started a small company, jobbing shipping supplies such as wrapping paper, bags, string, etc. The original Stone corporate office began with Joseph and his two sons all sharing one desk. In 1928 Joseph's youngest son, Jerome, joined the company. Also in 1928 the company started jobbing corrugated boxes, which became the product upon which today's company was built. During the Great Depression, J. H. Stone & Sons purchased five pieces of used equipment from another paper company for converting corrugated board into boxes, thus moving the company from jobber to manufacturer.

In the 1950s, jute linerboard was fast losing ground to kraft linerboard, which was lighter in weight and provided a stronger material for corrugated containers. This desire for a source of kraft linerboard led to the organization of South Carolina Industries, Inc. in Florence. Stone Container, in a joint venture with three other box manufacturers, arranged the financing, and construction began in 1962.

The Florence Mill began operation in 1963, signaling the company's entry into the production of kraft linerboard. While Stone was growing to become the world's largest producer of brown papers, the Florence Mill was also experiencing spectacular growth.

When the paper mill began operation, over 200 families came to this area from other locations to become employees of South Carolina Industries, because it was necessary to hire personnel with experience in the technical requirements of manufacturing paper. As these original employees left the area to work for other paper companies, they were replaced by area residents. All employees must start at the bottom and progress upward along lines of progression. New employees are under a constant training program to enable them to be promoted to a higher position as openings occur. At present, there are in excess of 550 employees, of which 43 are from the group originally hired.

Major expansions in 1974 and 1981 added two paper machines, a recycled fiber plant, four new batch digesters, and a black liquor recovery boiler. These expansions raised the mill production to its current level of more than 1,800 tons per day.

In 1981 Stone Container became the sole owner of the Florence Mill and changed its name from South Carolina Industries, Inc. to Stone Container Corporation, Florence Mill.

The Florence Mill began operating the first major cogeneration facility in the state in 1987. The facility generates an excess of electricity (approximately enough to supply the residential needs of the city of Florence) which is sold under contract to Carolina Power and Light Company.

Headquartered in Chicago, the company has manufacturing facilities and sales offices in North America, Europe, the United Kingdom, Central and South America, Australia, and the Pacific Rim.

Superior Machine Company of South Carolina, Inc.

Superior Machine Company, a homegrown industry which has extended its services into national and international markets, was founded in 1963 by Francis Marion Phillips (1927-96), a Georgia native who was, to a large extent, self-taught and self-made. Phillips' experience in machine engineering demonstrated that there was no adequate machine shop to service the rapidly expanding industrial base of the Florence area and, with backing of prospective customers, built one.

A disastrous fire in 1967, which destroyed the company's machinery and buildings, threatened its initial success. Undaunted, and with the encouragement and financial assistance of former customers, Phillips rebuilt. In 1983, when he sold the business, there were 135 employees. Superior was doing most of the work for southeastern paper and steel mills and beginning to expand overseas in the steel industry.

A leveraged buy-out of Superior was concluded January 13, 1983, by Bryan Jackson and a group of senior members of management, which included Hans Laufer, Elwood (Woody) Cunningham, and Wayne Pipkin. Subsequently, Wayne Walker and James Odom joined the ranks of owner/managers.

In July, 1983, Superior Machine Co. of South Carolina, Inc. acquired Marion Machine Company of Marion, North Carolina, the largest repair facility for rock crushers in the country, and probably the world.

Superior's principal markets, aside from the aggregate industries served by Marion, include the steel industry, where it is the largest manufacturer of equipment for remelting scrap steel, principally in minimills such as Nucor. The company specializes in the fabrication and rebuilding of electric arc furnaces, water-cooled roof and panel systems, and pollution control ductwork.

Servicing the pulp and paper industry gave Superior a start, and it continues to excel in the manufacture and rebuilding of wood chippers and chipper hardware, chip feeders, and woodyard equipment. It is Ingersoll-Rand Impco Division's only outside authorized repair facility, servicing thick stock and CloveRotor pumps and a wide array of other products. A recent joint venture was established with Columbia-based Dieter Bryce, Inc. to manufacture and market a revolutionary product called a cradle debarker, used for stripping bark from trees in preparation for processing the wood into paper.

Superior Machine Company also has entered the recycling industry. It has developed a series of heavy-duty wood waste grinders and entered into a long-term contract with a German company to manufacture shears, shredders, and compactors for recycling of automobiles and scrap metal, both in the United States and overseas.

Serving four diverse markets, as well as engaging in the repair and rebuilding of equipment, Superior Machine Company has maintained its policy of steady, balanced growth to protect loyal, competent employees from job insecurity, provide them with opportunities for advancement, and secure a reasonable return on the shareholders' investment.

Superior has taken numerous education initiatives in the Florence area, which include adopting local schools and providing financial assistance for special needs, service by management and employees on boards and councils of educational institutions, providing speakers and plant tours for schools on request, and making financial contributions. Bryan Jackson set an example by participating in civic affairs, having served as a past president of the Florence Chamber of Commerce and being named by it as "Business Person of the Year" in 1986.

Florence-Darlington Technical College

Florence-Darlington Technical College (FDTC) had as its beginning Senator Ernest F. Hollings' interest in technical education as a way to improve the job skills of South Carolina's workforce. It was his hope that skilled workers would attract industry to the state. His appointment in 1961 (while governor) of a legislative committee charged with investigating the possibility of establishing a statewide technical education system led to the creation of the state technical college system. In little more than 30 years, the system has grown to include 16 colleges located throughout the state. The system now boasts that nearly one out of two undergraduates in the state is enrolled in one of its institutions.

Florence-Darlington Technical College's 5000 Building

FDTC first opened its doors in March 1964, with less than 260 students and nearly 40,000 square feet of industrial/trade, classroom, and administrative office space. Established to serve the technical education needs of Florence, Darlington, and Marion Counties, the college was initially named the Florence-Darlington Technical Education Center. In 1974, after receiving accreditation from the Southern Association of Colleges and Schools (SACS), the college shortened its name to Florence-Darlington Technical College. The enrollment has almost doubled during the past eight years and now stands at 3,200 curriculum students. Its original campus of less than 10 acres has now expanded to nearly 100 acres with a modern complex of seven major buildings totaling nearly 300,000 square feet. The college's library houses nearly 30,000 books and offers students access to several on-line databases. The library contains strong technical, medical, and legal collections.

FDTC currently employs around 210 full-time people. About 112 of these full-time employees are faculty members. Fred C. Fore was president from 1964 to 1987; Dr. Michael B. McCall from 1988 to 1993; and Dr. Charles W. Gould is now president.

FDTC has–for a long time–been recognized as a major contributor to the economic health of the Pee Dee area. More than 60 degree, diploma, and certificate programs prepare FDTC students to meet the technical needs of area business and industry. In 1990 the college received approval from the Commission on Higher Education (CHE) to offer the associate of arts and associate of science degrees. These degrees make it possible for students to transfer to four-year institutions without losing credits.

Civil Engineering Technology students watch a computer-assisted design (CAD) demonstration.

FDTC's Continuing Education Division focuses on offering specialized training to meet the needs of business and industry. This division also offers general interest courses to the public. Computer, health, and business courses have been popular in recent years. In 1995 nearly 10,000 students took a course in FDTC's Continuing Education Division. FDTC operates a satellite campus in Hartsville, South Carolina, and courses are taught at this facility located on South Fourth Street near the Hartsville Mall.

The college's Special Schools Office handles workforce training for businesses and industries that are planning to locate in South Carolina or for existing industries that are creating new jobs. The Special Schools' component of the State Technical Education System is a model for demonstrating a state's effectivenes in recruiting industry. In recent years, Special Schools was instrumental in attracting BMW and Roche Carolina, Inc. to South Carolina.

Florence Carpet & Tile

In January, 1964, with hopes of a better future, lots of ambition, and despite limited capital, Charles and Barbara Carnell, along with George W. Jordan Jr., founded Florence Carpet & Linoleum, Inc. With very little money, the struggling business was operated from a telephone and desk located in a bedroom in the Carnells' home. Managing a business at home proved to be very difficult with two small children and another on the way. Job estimating and sales had to be done at night with days reserved for installation, which was done by Charles and the company's first employee, Armstrong "Shorty" Howard. With difficulty meeting financial obligations that continued for the first several years, it was necessary that payment for work completed be collected before any of the company's debts could be paid. Still, the company survived and, in late 1964, moved into its first office and showroom, a small 1,500-square-foot building located at the corner of Pamplico Highway and Purvis Drive. This move proved adequate for only a short while for the struggling, yet growing, company. A year later, additional warehouse space was added, followed by a showroom addition in 1967 that doubled the original building's space.

Shown above is the company's current 28,000-square-foot facility. Plans are underway for another addition in the near future.

The year 1969 brought two significant changes in the company. It was in that year that Mr. Jordan's share of the company was bought by the Carnells, and the company's name was changed. In the 1960s, inlaid linoleum was one of the most popular floor covering materials available, which is why it was included in Barbara's suggested name for the company. But with changes in the industry and with ceramic tile distribution becoming an important part of the business, the company's name was changed to the present one: Florence Carpet & Tile. This name had several advantages over the old one–it was shorter, easier to spell, and it better reflected what the company was about.

Moderate growth in the 1960s progressed to tremendous growth in the early 1970s. With this growth came the need for more space. In 1974 construction was begun on a new location one block from the original, and on July 4, 1974, the business moved into its new 21,000-square-foot warehouse and showroom.

The recession of the middle 1970s slowed down both business and growth, but the company once again survived hard times. Growth picked up considerably in the decade that followed, and in 1987, another building addition increased space to 28,000 square feet.

The future looks bright for Florence Carpet & Tile with another expansion planned within the next two years. Throughout 32 years, two locations, numerous industry awards, and a name change later, its goals remain the same: To sell quality products and services at reasonable prices, to stand behind its products and workmanship, and to give recognition to dedicated and dependable employees. With these goals, Florence Carpet & Tile has grown from a small, in-home operation to a regional leader in the residential and commercial interior industry. It is also with these goals that the company looks to its future.

This showroom addition in 1967 doubled the original building's previous space.

ESAB Welding & Cutting Products

The Florence plant of ESAB began operations as part of the Linde Division of Union Carbide in 1966. In 1985 Union Carbide sold this business to a limited partnership, and the new business was named L-TEC Welding &

Since developing the plasma process in the 1950s, ESAB has introduced many innovations that have kept its technologies and products at the forefront of the industry and established ESAB as the plasma market leader.

Cutting Systems. The Florence plant became a part of the ESAB Group, the world's largest welding and cutting company, in 1989. In 1994 the ESAB Group became part of Charter PLC, a publicly held company in the United Kingdom. With annual sales of over one billion dollars, The ESAB Group is the leading producer of welding and cutting solutions in the world.

The Florence plant has gone through considerable expansion, and over 400 jobs were added to it when operations at facilities in Indiana, New Jersey, Illinois, and Colorado were moved here. Ray Hoglund is the president and CEO of ESAB Welding & Cutting Products, North America, with corporate offices located in Florence.

The Florence operation is one of numerous ESAB manufacturing facilities located in this country and worldwide. The products are sold through more than 1,300 distributors in the United States and through country companies and distributors around the world. More than 20 percent of the products made in Florence are exported.

The products designed, engineered, and manufactured by ESAB in Florence include regulators, torches, and related oxy-fuel cutting and welding equipment; Mig, Tig, and Plasma torches, wire feeders, and power sources for electric arc welding and plasma cutting; automated cutting systems; and products for the steel industry.

ESAB is one of the largest employers in the Florence area. It has approximately 1,000 employees and adds over $50 million to the local economy each year. There are jobs in engineering which require a BS, MS degree; jobs in data processing which require either a BS, MS, or a technology degree in computer programming with work experience; jobs in accounting; jobs in management; in manufacturing; and other support staff. The production systems used are the latest technology and utilize state-of-the-art manufacturing techniques. The Florence facility has approximately 50,000 square feet of floor space which includes the following:

- North American corporate head quarters and financial services
- Engineering and development labs for product design and development
- Marketing and customer service offices
- Computer related systems support group
- Customer demonstrations and training center

And Manufacturing operations such as:

- Plastic Molding
- Nozzle Swagging
- Sheet Metal Stamping
- Plating
- Transformer Winding
- Machine Assembly
- Painting
- Testing
- Welding
- Packaging
- Machining
- Brazing

The men and women at ESAB are proud that their contributions and workmanship establish the excellence of products manufactured in the Florence plant throughout the world. They take part in many civic, sporting, and cultural activities in the Florence area. They support these community activities both through corporate and

One of the pioneers in Mig welding systems. ESAB's technical knowledge of Mig arcs and systems technology is recognized as producing the finest Mig performance available.

individual volunteer efforts. ESAB is one of the proud sponsors of the Ben Hogan Golf Tournament held each year in Florence. They carry on the tradition of innovation, engineering excellence, and quality control that has made ESAB the world leader in the welding and cutting industry.

Francis Marion University

Francis Marion University was the first degree-granting college created by the South Carolina Legislature in the twentieth century. The impetus for creating a college in the Pee Dee region began in the Florence Kiwanis Club. Dr. J. Howard Stokes (1909-78), James Rogers (1905-90), Clifford Cormell, and John Kassab initiated the efforts to persuade the governor of the overwhelming need for a state-supported institution of higher learning in the Pee Dee. As a result, in 1957 the University of South Carolina established a "freshman center" at the Florence County Library. A year later, a sophomore class was added.

The J. Howard Stokes Administration Building was the first building constructed on the campus.

By 1961 a permanent campus for the USC-Florence branch was established east of Florence at Mars Bluff. One hundred acres, including an antebellum-style house (Wallace Hall), was donated by the Wallace family and now serves as the president's home (called Wallace House). The first building constructed was the J. Howard Stokes Administration Building.

The enrollment at the campus reached 350 by 1966, an indication that the institution would expand to a four-year college. In 1969 the legislature created Francis Marion College, named for General Francis Marion, famed Revolutionary War hero.

Dr. Walter Douglas Smith accepted the presidency of the new college in September, 1969, with an enrollment of 906 students for the 1970 opening fall session. Enrollment increased to 1,443 in 1971. In the next few years, campus acreage tripled and five buildings were added: the James A. Rogers Library, the Robert E. McNair Science Building, the Walter Douglas Smith University Center, Founders Hall, and the John K. Cauthen Educational Media Center.

Upon Smith's retirement in 1983, Dr. Thomas C. Stanton became president. Physical growth continued in the 1980s with the addition of the Peter D. Hyman Fine Arts Center, apartment complex and dormitory housings, Edward S. Ervin III Dining Hall, and the Thomas C. Stanton Academic Computer Center. In 1992 construction included the Hugh K. Leatherman Sr. Science Facility. Also in 1992 the state legislature granted university status to the college, and the name changed to Francis Marion University. In the fall of 1993, enrollment reached 4,103. Stanton retired in 1994 and was succeeded by Dr. Lee A. Vickers.

Today, the university offers four undergraduate degrees: Bachelor of Arts, Bachelor of Business Administration, Bachelor of General Studies, and Bachelor of Science. Graduate degrees are offered in applied psychology, business administration, and education. Twenty-eight majors are available in addition to cooperative programs with other institutions and several pre-professional programs.

Under the leadership of President Vickers, the university increased access to technological services (Internet and satellite service), expanded course offerings, increased student development opportunities with an emphasis on a student-centered learning environment, and extended community outreach programs. The university has graduates from every county in South Carolina, 32 other states, Puerto Rico, and 22 foreign countries.

The athletic program is a member of the NCAA Division II Peach Belt Athletic Conference and sponsors 14 intercollegiate sports.

Francis Marion contributes significantly to the quality of life in Florence through efforts in continuing education, technical and professional assistance, and artistic, literary, and scientific programs offered to the public. As one of the area's largest employers, the university has a major economic impact in the community.

ABB Power T&D Company Inc.

At home in Florence–and all around the world

The Florence plant of ABB Distribution Systems Division was erected in 1979 by its original owner, BBC Brown Boveri. Its rich heritage in the electric power industry was rooted in a pioneering company called ITE, founded in 1927. In 1987 BBC merged with Asea, a Swedish firm, to create Asea Brown Boveri, now called ABB. Distribution Systems Division is now part of ABB Power T&D Company, headquartered in Raleigh, North Carolina.

As a $33-billion corporation with over 200,000 employees, ABB is the largest company in the world to focus on electric power generation, transmission and distribution. ABB is at home in Florence, and all around the world.

In Florence, ABB designs and manufactures circuit breakers rated from 480 volts up to 38,000 volts for utility and industrial customers in the United States and all over the world. ABB circuit breakers are used to control electricity and protect power distribution systems and customer equipment in applications ranging from utility and industrial substations to nuclear power plants. The ISO-9001 certified plant also produces interrupter switches and the Kirk™ line of safety interlocks. The 150,000-square-foot facility has extensive laser cutting, CNC machining and plating systems to support the fabrication of intricate, precision parts for circuit breakers, and is home to engineering, manufacturing and marketing personnel.

Companies often claim that people are their most important asset. ABB "walks the talk." Over 90 production employees are organized into self-directed work teams. No middle management is present to bog down communications. Using extensive training in job skills, team building and TQM tools, the self-directed work teams are responsible for their own daily scheduling, problem solving, cost reductions and quality. The result: ABB products are manufactured by the most involved, motivated and responsible workforce available anywhere.

Computer controlled production testing of new ADVAC™ circuit breaker.

Global technology leadership

ABB product development is founded on world-class technology created from $120 million annually in R&D in this business area alone. Locally, world-class engineering talent is supported by the latest design and test systems, such as finite element analysis, three-dimensional modeling and digital test equipment. ABB innovation has resulted in the most compact and highest performance circuit breakers in the industry, as well as the new ADVAC™ advanced design vacuum circuit breaker.

From technology leadership to community leadership

Florence is a great place for a manufacturing business, offering a diverse and dedicated workforce, technical education, a supportive family environment and excellent access by interstate highways, air, rail and nearby ports.

In turn, ABB supports Florence through its wage base, purchases from local suppliers, educational opportunities and challenges for the personal and career growth of its employees. Civic-minded employees further support the community by selfless participation in United Way fund drives and countless other activities. And the Florence facility will soon become the U.S. test site for ABB implementation of ISO-14000, the world standard for environmental responsibility.

The future of ABB in Florence is bright, with success coming from new products, active local markets and increasing export opportunities. ABB is clearly the long-term partner for global power distribution, acting in a long-term partnership with the Florence community.

Engineer using high speed video to analyze motion in circuit breaker mechanism.

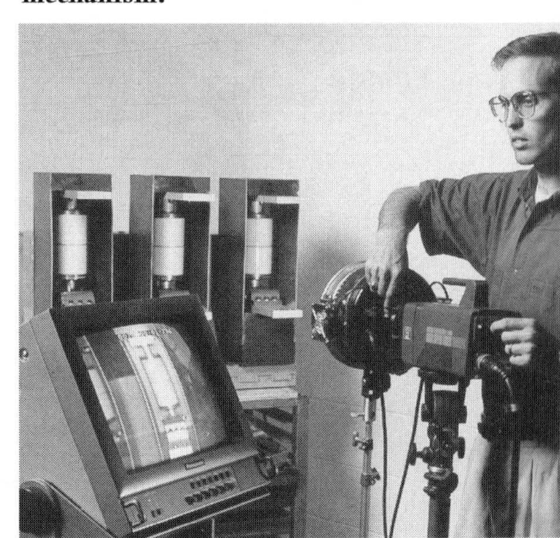

Turner, Padget, Graham & Laney, P.A.

The law firm of Turner, Padget, Graham & Laney, P.A. traces its beginnings back to May 1, 1929, when Nathaniel A. (Nat) Turner announced the opening of an office for the general practice of law in Columbia, South Carolina. Over the next 55 years, the firm grew to become one of the largest firms in the state, with approximately 20 attorneys. In 1984, to accommodate the legal needs of a major client in Florence, and also due to the perceived growth potential of the Pee Dee area, the firm opened its first "branch" office in Florence. One of the firm's partners, John Wilkerson, moved his family and practice to Florence and opened an office on October 29, 1984.

The firm's Florence partners *(L to R):* Art Justice, Wayne Byrd, John Wilkerson, and Hugh Claytor. *Photo by Allen Gibson*

The first location was a small office in a newly constructed building at 1807 Cherokee Road. The firm's confidence in the Florence economy was not misplaced, because in 1987 they had grown to six attorneys and moved to a suite of offices in the Florence Business and Technology Center. Another change occurred in 1990 when the firm moved to its current location in the BB&T (formerly Southern National Bank) building on the corner of Cashua and West Evans Streets. Their commitment to Florence is reflected in the fact that the firm became a one-third owner of the building. They have now grown to 11 attorneys with 13 support staff in the Florence office. Other state-wide law firms have followed Turner Padget's lead, and now there are at least four satellite law offices located in Florence. The firm has also continued to grow throughout the state with 38 attorneys in Columbia and a newly established Charleston office.

Turner, Padget, Graham & Laney has distinguished itself in the Florence community as well as on the state and national level. They have been active participants in the Greater Florence Chamber of Commerce where Art Justice served as chairman in 1993-94. Other local organizations include Florence County Progress, Pee Dee Economic Development Partnership, United Way of Florence, and many more. Their partners include a past president of the South Carolina Bar, and a past president of the South Carolina Defense Trial Attorneys' Association, members of the Board of Governors and House of Delegates of the South Carolina Bar, and a regional vice president of the Defense Research Institute. Members of the firm are also active in national defense organizations, including Defense Research Institute (DRI), International Association of Defense Counsel (IADC), and Federation of Insurance and Corporate Counsel (FICC).

Turner, Padget, Graham & Laney provides a wide range of services to its clients including litigation, business enterprises, and employment law. *Photo by Allen Gibson*

Clients of the firm include some of the largest employers in South Carolina and represent a diverse range of business and legal interests, including manufacturers, financial institutions, health care providers, developers, retailers, governmental units, insurance companies, and many others. Turner Padget's areas of practice include administrative law, alternative dispute resolution, banking and creditor's rights, commercial litigation, construction law, corporate/real estate, employment law, environmental law, governmental affairs, health care, insurance and tort litigation, insurance regulation, professional negligence, products liability, and workers' compensation.

Amana

Located along I-95 in the Florence Industrial Park is the Amana Plant which makes a full line of home cooking products–gas and electric ranges, cooktops, and wall ovens. The plant has approximately 650 employees and produces over 200,000 units per year which are shipped to homes all over the world.

The Amana Corporation began as the Caloric Corporation. The roots of the Caloric Corporation were planted in Philadelphia in 1889 with the founding of Klein Stove Company. This venture, initially devoted to the fabrication of wood and coal burning stoves, established the base for what has today become one of the leading major appliance design, manufacturing, and marketing operations in the nation.

Near the turn of the century, the company began to specialize in gas burning ranges; and in 1903 Caloric–an ancient word for heat–was first used by the company.

During World War I Caloric acquired the old Topton Foundry and Machine Company. In the years that followed, Caloric operated out of three separate Pennsylvania locations. In 1941 all operations were centralized at the original foundry site in Topton.

Caloric developed rapidly in the years following World War II, establishing itself as the leading gas range manufacturing company in the northeastern United States.

It wasn't until 1966, when Raytheon Company acquired Caloric, that the company diversified its product line and became a national marketer of major kitchen appliances.

In 1973 Caloric introduced its first electric range line. In 1978 Caloric acquired the Glenwood Range Company, one of America's oldest stove manufacturers; and in 1981 Modern Maid Company, which traced its heritage to 1904.

In 1987 Caloric Corporation expanded its manufacturing base and built a 422,000-square-foot plant in Florence. The plant opened its offices here in July, 1988, and by January of 1989, the first production employees were working at the new facility. In July, 1989, the first range was completed on the production lines, and Caloric was on its way to becoming a major employer in the region.

Caloric gas stove

Amana, Florence Operations

Topton Manufacturing Plant

A commitment to quality products and a dedicated, outstanding, and involved workforce point to continued success for Amana. The Amana plant is truly a vital part of the Florence community, and its employees are committed to "making a difference." ❧

The new facility continued producing quality ranges and in 1991 Caloric Corporation decided to close its manufacturing operations in Topton, Pennsylvania, and relocate all manufacturing and corporate facilities to Florence. Once again, change was in the air as floors were taken up and walls relocated and machinery from Pennsylvania began to be moved into the building. New employees and new products began to show up in the plant. By mid-1991, employment had increased to 750 people, and the future was very promising.

From 1991 to 1993, Caloric continued to consolidate its position in the marketplace, and in June, 1993, the parent company, Raytheon Company, announced that the Caloric Corporation would be consolidated with the Amana Corporation to form one company under the Amana name.

Today, the plant continues to produce top-of-the-line cooking products under the brand names of Amana and Caloric, along with specialty products for other manufacturers. The future looks particularly bright as major products will receive significant design improvements that will bring the modern home into the twenty-first century.

Electric free-standing range

DARLINGTON
74
Lipton
Lipton TEA 74
57
BUDGET GOURMET
BUDGET GOURMET 57
95
CATERPILLAR
CAT

Kitchens!

In the fall of 1982, a series of events occurred which were to result in the creation of Kitchens!, a kitchen and bath dealership combined with a gourmet cook's shop. Kitchens! co-owner, Agnes Heinitsh Willcox, active member of the Florence County Historical Commission and Florence Heritage Foundation, sought and found a Victorian home in Darlington which could be moved and restored on property in the Country Club section of Florence. It seemed a perfect house–except the space to be used for the kitchen was a complicated combination of oversized windows, doorways, and fireplace. Agnes began studying the techniques of kitchen design in order to design the space to suit her catering business activities, and to have a kitchen appropriate for an 1889 Victorian home. This new interest soon replaced catering, and several years later, combined with volunteer involvement to form a partnership known as Kitchens! The owners of Kitchens! got to know each other through their Junior League volunteer work and decided to begin a business venture together.

The Willcox Residence, c. 1889. Formerly the Edwards House, this home was moved from Darlington and restored in Florence in 1984. It is currently located in Country Club Estates.

While serving as president of the Florence Junior League, Agnes worked with fellow volunteer Elizabeth Gaskin on a new project–moving and restoring an historic house to be used as a headquarters for the League. This project was brought to fruition two years later when Elizabeth was president of the Junior League. Kitchens! opened in October of 1990 and began its first year in the Florence Mall. That same fall, Kitchens! designed the kitchen in Florence's Women's Symphony Guild's first Designer Showhouse, and has since been invited to participate in five other Designer Showhouses–three in Florence, two in Charleston, and one in Camden. With business growing steadily, Kitchens! moved its location to 1811 Cherokee Road, just beside the intersection at Five Points. Having designed and installed over 75 kitchens and baths since the business opened, Agnes has gone on to receive the designation of Certified Kitchen Designer and is an affiliate member of ASID. Kitchens! does remodeling and is a member of the National Kitchen & Bath Association, the National Association of Homebuilders, and the Florence Chamber of Commerce. Elizabeth currently serves on the board of the Chamber.

An intense interest in historic preservation has led the partners to expand their business into moving and restoring old homes for sale. In addition, Agnes and Elizabeth were project managers for the restoration of the Summer Academy at Pawleys Island and, in Florence, of the Columns, the Johnson/Harwell home. Agnes designed and oversaw the installation of the kitchens in both homes, insuring that the rooms were appropriately preserved while functioning as modern-day facilities.

Kitchens! carries fine custom cabinets as well as unusual pieces of distressed and antiqued painted furniture, heart pine mantles, a full array of kitchen gadgets, gourmet cookware, decorative accessories such as unusual ceramic platters and canisters, colorful linens, and much more.

In 1995 Kitchens! expanded its full-service kitchen and bath design and installation business from DeBordieu to Myrtle Beach, the Pee Dee region, the Columbia and Lake Murray area, and to North Carolina, in the mountain resort of Lake Toxaway. ❧

The Willcox Residence, c. 1893, was moved from Pine Street to Sheffield Estates in 1994. The home was designed by Florence Architect, Silas Bounds, for his daughter.

Roche Carolina Inc.

A 1,400-acre site near the junction of Route 301/76 and East Old Marion Highway is the home of one of Florence's newest corporate citizens–Roche Carolina Inc. The arrival of Roche Carolina underscores the emergence of Florence as a major health care center and home to several high-technology companies.

Roche Carolina is a wholly owned subsidiary of Hoffmann-La Roche Inc. of Nutley, New Jersey, which is a U.S. affiliate of the multinational group of companies headed by Roche Holding Ltd. of Basel, Switzerland.

One of the world's leading research-intensive health care companies, Roche has discovered, developed, and marketed numerous important prescription pharmaceuticals. It is also a major provider of diagnostic products and services as well as vitamins and other products for human and animal nutrition and health. Recognized for excellence in both biotechnology and chemistry, Roche is also widely known for its current efforts in the research, development, and commercialization of polymerase chain reaction (PCR) technology, a revolutionary advance in diagnostics and other fields, including biomedical research, forensics, and environmental testing.

Roche Carolina's research and development operations are situated in the Pharmaceutical Technical Center, which consists of two buildings: the two-story, 82,000-square-foot Laboratory Building, *foreground*, and the five-story, 90,000-square-foot Pilot Plant, *background*. *Photo by Cramer Gallimore Photography.*

Roche is pursuing a strategy of focusing its powerful pharmaceutical research and development (R&D) capability on the search for innovative products for unmet health care needs. Roche Carolina will play a key role in helping the company attain this goal in three ways:

- by developing processes to "scale up" the manufacture of new medications from the research laboratory to mass production,
- by producing quantities of pharmaceutical active ingredients for medium-and large-sized clinical trials of experimental compounds, and
- by producing bulk quantities of the active ingredients used in new pharmaceuticals. Active ingredients produced by the Florence operation will be shipped to Roche finished dosage form production facilities worldwide, where they will be pressed into tablets, filled into capsules, and converted into other dosage forms.

When completed, the Florence facility will bring Roche closer to achieving a "time to market" production strategy, whereby the company will have similar pharmaceutical R&D and bulk manufacturing facilities in Basel, Switzerland, and Florence. These interchangeable facilities will help Roche bring its pharmaceuticals to market faster and with outstanding quality and cost efficiency.

The master plan calls for development of approximately one half of Roche Carolina's 1,400-acre site, leaving significant amounts of land between the facility and its neighbors. The site is being developed in phases. Construction on the project began in 1992. Phase I was completed in mid-1996, and the second phase of construction is under way.

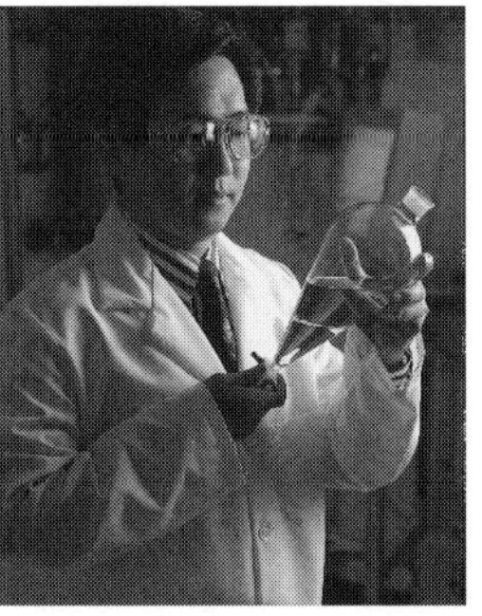

Roche Carolina has a diverse work force united by the common goal of bringing safe, effective, and innovative new medications to market in an expeditious manner. Joe Chou, Ph.D., a research investigator with more than 15 years of process engineering experience, is helping develop a new cancer drug. *Photo by Van Miller.*

The centerpiece of Phase I is the Pharmaceutical Technical Center (PTC), where R&D operations are conducted. The PTC consists of a two-story, 82,000-square-foot Laboratory Building and a five-story, 90,000-square-foot Pilot Plant. Also in Phase I are a site services building, a visitors center, and related infrastructure, including an energy center, a waste water pretreatment plant, a warehouse, and three miles of road.

Phase II consists of additional infrastructure and a seven-story, 340,000-square-foot structure known as the Launch Facility, where bulk quantities of pharmaceutical active ingredients will be produced. Phase II is scheduled for completion in 1997 and will become operational in 1998.

Many South Carolina firms have

been involved in the construction of Roche Carolina. As of the spring of 1996, Roche Carolina had awarded contracts worth more than $65 million to South Carolina companies, approximately $15 million of which have gone to firms based in Florence County. Roche Carolina has also actively sought out and hired minority-owned companies to work on the project.

Roche Carolina is being built, and will operate, in an environmentally sensitive fashion. Roche is investing approximately $80 million in environmental and safety features for the Florence site. For example, waste water is pretreated on-site before it is discharged into the city of Florence treatment system; the most advanced technology available is being used for controlling and monitoring air emissions; and culverts carry storm water

The Pharmaceutical Technical Center (building with atrium skylight) is the centerpiece of Phase I construction, which was completed in mid-1996. The seven-story, 340,000-square-foot Launch Facility, *background*, where bulk quantities of pharmaceutical active ingredients will be made, is the centerpiece of Phase II construction, which is scheduled for completion in 1997. *Photo by Cramer Gallimore Photography.*

to an on-site containment pond. The water is tested and treated, if necessary, before it's discharged.

When the first two phases of construction are completed, Roche Carolina will employ approximately 300 people, many of whom will be hired locally. A key source of highly skilled technical employees is the Special Schools program of the South Carolina State Board for Technical and Comprehensive Education. Special Schools has partnered with Roche Carolina to train more than 75 technical employees who were later hired by the company. As the need arises, Special Schools will train additional technical employees to work at Roche Carolina.

Development of a diverse and flexible workforce is key to Roche Carolina's team-based work environment. Employees are united by the mission of speeding the development of important new compounds in Roche's global pharmaceuticals portfolio–promising medications for AIDS, Alzheimer's, Parkinson's, cancer, and other insidious diseases.

In keeping with Roche's corporate focus on the environment, health care, and education, particularly in mathematics and the sciences, Roche Carolina has developed community relations partnerships in South Carolina. To date, Roche has formalized educational partnerships with:

- University of South Carolina;
- Clemson University;
- Francis Marion University;
- Florence Darlington Technical College;
- South Carolina State Board for Technical and Comprehensive Education;
- South Carolina Business Center for Excellence in Education;
- Governor's School for Science and Mathematics; and
- Florence Public School District Number One.

Roche Carolina is committed to being a good corporate citizen that supports the community in which it operates. The company believes in developing shared goals with others, including its employees and business and community partners.

Creating an environment that fosters interaction and creativity among scientific personnel was a key objective in the design of Roche Carolina's Pharmaceutical Technical Center. Communication "nodules" in a sun-and plant-filled atrium lobby serve as informal meeting places. *Photo by Van Miller.*

Roche Carolina and its employees are involved in a host of civic, social service, and charitable activities in the greater Florence area. Roche strongly encourages community service and matches the commitment of employees with financial support.

As Roche Carolina moves from the construction to the operational phase, the company will continue to build upon the relationships it has established as well as develop new ones.

Bibliography

Brunson, W. A. *Reminiscences of Reconstruction in Darlington* Hartsville: The Pee Dee Historical Society, 1910.

Centennial Essays. *Florence Morning News*, 1989-1990.
Hux, Roger K. "Florence Library Association."
Rudisill, Horace Fraser. "Plantations in the City of Florence."
Simpson, Robert R. and Prince, Eldred E. Jr. "Frank Mandeville Rogers."
Zeigler, Benjamin T. "Confederate Cruiser *Pedee*,"
"Confederate Stockade at Florence,"
"Skirmish at Gamble's Hotel."
Zeigler, Eugene N. (numerous articles).

Davis, Henry E. "History of Florence: City and County."

King, G. Wayne. *Rise Up So Early*. Spartanburg: Reprint Company, 1981.

McNeil, J. P. and John A. Chase. *Florence County: Economic and Social*. Columbia: University of South Carolina, 1921.

Price, Julian P. *That Little Old Doctor Tells a Story*. Charlotte: Delmar, 1985.

Rudisill, Horace Fraser. *The Diaries of Evan Pugh*. Florence: St. David's Society, 1993.

South Carolina: A Guide to the Palmetto State. New York: Oxford University Press, 1941.

Swanton, John R. *The Indians of the Southeastern United States*. Washington, D.C.: U.S. Government Printing Office, 1945.

Wallace, D. D. *The History of South Carolina*. New York: The American Historical Society, Inc., 1934.

Acknowledments

Any written history worth reading requires the assistance of many people. The author is indebted to Horace Fraser Rudisill, Benjamin T. Zeigler, and Dr. G. Wayne King for reading the manuscript and making helpful editorial suggestions and factual corrections. Eleanor E. McMahan rendered invaluable service in proofing and correcting the manuscript in its various stages of composition. The photographs which have been used come largely from the collection of Dr. G. Wayne King. Jane Jackson gave permission to use some of her sketches and watercolors and Larry McLaughlin consented to the use of two of Jane's watercolors on which he owns the copyright. Howard S. Waddell furnished many of the railroad pictures used. Last, but not least, I am indebted to my wife for her patience, forbearance, and encouragement while I wrote this history in my "spare time."

Eugene N. Zeigler

Enterprises Index

Index

This book was set in Baskerville, Bellevue, Bodoni, Copperplate Gothic, and Ellington at Community Communications in Montgomery, Alabama